SOLANO
COMMUNITY COLLEGE

Donation by

RISING
TO THE
CHALLENGE

RISING TO THE CHALLENGE

THE AUTOBIOGRAPHY OF KOJI KOBAYASHI

Harcourt Brace Jovanovich Japan
Tokyo, Japan

HARCOURT BRACE JOVANOVICH JAPAN, INC.
Ichibancho Central Bldg., 22-1, Ichibancho, Chiyoda-ku, Tokyo 102

ISBN4-8337-0502-8

Printed in Japan
89 90 91 92 9 8 7 6 5 3 2 1

CONTENTS

CONTENTS

CONTENTS

PREFACE TO THE
ENGLISH EDITION

On May 25, 1988, two months after *Watashi no Rirekisho* (My Personal History) was published in Japanese by the *Nihon Keizai Shimbun,* I retired as chairman of the board of NEC and became chairman emeritus and representative director. This volume has therefore come to assume a special significance for me. Unlike the six other books of mine that have appeared since 1968, this one is a highly subjective account of my life as a private individual, my contributions as an engineer to NEC, and my years at the helm as its chief executive officer. Perhaps for that very reason I have received many letters since its publication, from colleagues and friends and even from readers I have never met, sharing their recollections and offering words of encouragement.

For the Japanese edition of this first attempt at autobiography, I chose the subtitle "From the Mountains of Japan to the World Stage." And in accordance with this I tried to organize the events of my life to show how, by challenging and overcoming the status quo, I emerged from the village at the foot of Mount Fuji where I was born 82 years ago to establish a place for myself in international society. Perhaps mine has not been an exceptional life, and if typically Japanese ways of thinking or patterns of behavior can be found on every page, these are the inevitable reflections of myself as a Japanese. But today, when NEC does business with over 140 countries and our ties with people the world over have grown steadily deeper, I hope that this account of the experience of a Japanese business executive may be of interest to an English-speaking audience.

When I first started working in the field of communications engineering, I dreamed that one day we would be able to pick up a telephone and talk to anyone, anywhere, at any time, and that I might contribute in some way to making that day possible. In the near future, information networks facilitating the free exchange of ideas will become an established part of the social infrastructure. My dreams, it seems, are about to become reality.

As an omen perhaps of things to come, trends in the economy today are substantially changing the meaning of national boundaries. Although economic tension among the advanced industrial countries has emerged as a serious problem, perhaps this tension results from the strain between two mutually antagonistic principles—the globalism of today's economic world and the nationalism of the political world. If this is the case, we must not yield to the temptations of nationalism, but each of us should try to find solutions to the problems that confront us by reexamining our country's position and role in international society. It is my firm conviction that desirable change may spring from the collective hopes and aspirations of individual men and women throughout the world.

In June 1987, when I had the honor to be guest lecturer at the precommencement exercises of New York University's Graduate School of Business Administration, I stated my belief that only by correctly assessing the current state of affairs and taking the appropriate actions can the United States and Japan achieve mutual prosperity. But this formula is not limited to Japanese-American relations. For the peoples of the world who, in the forty-odd years since the end of World War II, have climbed step by arduous step out of the depths of poverty with their eyes fixed on the promising skies ahead, such a constructive partnership is a beacon to guide them on the road that lies before them. We should not regard their emergence on the world stage with hostility or malice but with encouragement and sympathetic good will.

With the publication of the English translation of my autobiography, I would like to express my deepest thanks to Professor Ryuzo Sato, director of the Center of Japan-U.S. Business and Economic Studies at New York University, for his useful advice and assistance; to the translator, Mrs. Jean Hoff; to Junichiro

Minagawa of Harcourt Brace Jovanovich Japan; and to all those both in Japan and the United States whose efforts have made this book possible.

Koji Kobayashi
May 1989
Tokyo, Japan

PREFACE TO THE
JAPANESE EDITION

Every forty years the world faces a major turning point. This is a long-held belief of mine. Perhaps this pattern is only an accident of recent history, but forty years does seem to be an appropriate interval over which to look back. I was born on February 17, 1907, not long after the Japan-Russia War, one such major turning point in modern Japanese history, and was raised in Yamanashi Prefecture, in a village at the northern foot of Mount Fuji. In the more than eighty years since then I have encountered regional barriers, corporate barriers, technological barriers, and national barriers, all of which, for the most part, I have succeeded in overcoming. My life has been a series of challenges that I have faced with enthusiasm and determination.

Still pursuing my dreams I reached my eightieth birthday in February 1987. Many people congratulated me on that occasion, and around that time I received a request from the *Nihon Keizai Shimbun* to contribute to its ongoing series "My Personal History." As I recall, the editors first asked me to write for them more than ten years ago, but because of my executive responsibilities, I kept turning them down. Finally I decided it would be rude to refuse any longer and set about to record the events of my life. The first installment appeared on November 1, 1987. To be honest, I enjoyed recalling the incidents of my youth and asked many of my colleagues to help me remember those bygone days. I would like to thank them here for their assistance.

The present book is a greatly revised and expanded version of the "My Personal History" columns first serialized in the *Nihon*

Keizai Shimbun. As such it is neither my own private memoirs nor an official history of the NEC Corporation—there are far too many digressions, I am afraid. Rather, the book is the personal account of one individual who, from the day he first entered the company, has devoted all of his energy and enthusiasm to NEC.

As I look back over my fifty-eight years in the company, I often find myself wondering what young people just entering NEC are thinking and how their concerns compare to my own of more than half a century ago. I cannot deny that the world has changed greatly since then. And yet something constant has remained untouched amid all these changes. I hope that the young people of today who will carry the hopes of the world into the twenty-first century will be able to grasp this unchanging constant. And if this small volume can help them do so, I will be very happy.

Koji Kobayashi
March 1988

RISING
TO THE
CHALLENGE

1

CHILDHOOD AND STUDENT DAYS

THE KOBAYASHI FAMILY OF HATSUKARI VILLAGE

In Japan a person's name is often considered his destiny. The name Kobayashi means "small forest"—the English equivalent might be Littlewood. Because this family name suggests a closed and confined space, the given name, it is said, must expand and open that space up. That is why my father chose the character for "wide" as part of my first name. One of my very earliest memories is hearing this story. I was deeply impressed by why I had been given the name Koji and often found myself wondering how I could rule widely over my own small forest.

For generations the Kobayashi family had had no direct male heirs and had perpetuated its name through adopted sons. But in my father's time we were a large family of five boys and four girls. When I was born, on February 17, 1907, I was the fourth son in the family.

My father Tsuneo was born into the Fujimoto family of Yanagawa Village in Yamanashi Prefecture, some fifty miles west of Tokyo. After graduating from the Kofu Gitenkan School in 1886, he became an elementary school teacher and served in my hometown of Hatsukari as the principal of the elementary school. He was said to have been a man of exceptional ability. Indeed, a Gitenkan classmate of his named Tamezo had written a Chinese poem in his praise. I still have the poem, but it is too difficult for me to read.

My father was adopted into the Kobayashi family when he married my mother Den. Den, the daughter of my grandfather Sataro and my grandmother Koto was heiress to the family estate. My father resigned as school principal when he succeeded my grandfather as head of the family.

My grandfather Sataro was the son of Busuke Maeda from a nearby village. He too had been adopted into the Kobayashi family through marriage. After his marriage he changed his name from Gitaro to Daisuke and assumed the name Sataro when my great-grandfather Sataro died. Grandfather Sataro had been born into a family of large landowners, who used to ride around on horseback to collect the land tax. When my grandfather was adopted by the Kobayashi family, he is said to have brought a sizable dowry with him.

After he became head of the family, Sataro acted as a broker dealing in silk thread and silk goods. Often he would head east across the Kobotoke Pass to Edo (modern-day Tokyo) or west through the Sasago Pass to Kofu, the capital of Yamanashi Prefecture. In those days bandits used to lie in ambush in these mountain passes. The strongest of them all went by the name of Akatsuki no Myojo—"Bright Star at Daybreak." My grandfather used to carry a pistol to protect himself, and the family still has a gun permit that dates back to 1881.

Sataro does not seem to have been satisfied with being a silk broker and he eventually set out for Kofu, where he tried his hand at silk manufacturing. This venture ended in failure, however, and he returned to Hatsukari. Back in the village he ran a small business, then retired, helping out occasionally on the farm. Near the end of his life he used to tell his grandchildren about the big business schemes that he had never been able to realize. This was before I entered school, so I have only vague recollections of what he said.

ELEMENTARY SCHOOL DAYS

Sports Day at the Hatsukari Elementary School, which I entered in 1913, was held once a year in the autumn. For my schoolmates and me it was the one truly enjoyable event of the year. I still can remember the words of our Sports Day song. On that day all the boys wore white flannel shirts and pants, which our parents no doubt made considerable sacrifices to buy. We wore those clothes for the rest of the year and waited impatiently for the next Sports Day to come around again.

When I entered school Japan's victory in the Japan-Russia War of 1904–5 was still fresh in people's memories. The sound of bells and the cries of a newsboy selling extra editions of the newspaper had been how we learned that the war hero General Maresuke Nogi had committed ritual suicide on the evening of the Emperor Meiji's funeral. Bayonets, trophies of the Japan-Russia War, were displayed in the entrance to my elementary school. And I can still remember the disabled war veterans who used to go from village to village selling medicines.

But the world of the past was changing. I was about five or six when we first got electric lights. Before then I had had to clean the glass chimney of the kerosene lamp every night, and I can remember how thrilled I was to be freed from this chore. Just about this time I also saw my first automobile. "There's an automobile!" I heard someone say, and I ran out into the garden. By then, however, the car was far away. All I saw was its taillights glowing in the distance like the eyes of a dragon.

The elementary school was right behind our house, only two or three minutes away. The principal, Mr. Jusei Asakawa, was a stern yet courteous man. I can still vividly recall his dignified appearance. In elementary school I was always class president. I was rather good at my studies, but poor at gymnastics and running. Perhaps because I have always been somewhat stout, I invariably came in second to last in footraces.

Almost every day we played tennis in the schoolyard or caught fish in the river that ran right in back of the school. We would reach under the rocks and catch bullheads, a type of goby, with our bare hands or use fishing rods to catch dace. Sometimes in the evenings we set out twenty or so fishing hooks, then woke up early the next morning and went down to the river to pull them up. Usually we would catch two or three eels that way. Eels were an important part of our diet.

Since ours was a poor village surrounded by mountains, getting enough protein was a serious problem. At the end of the year villagers would exchange gifts of salted salmon, which would then be hung over the hearth. Because salted salmon would keep for a year, it was a valuable source of nourishment. The households that had many salmon hanging over their hearths were generally the richest and of the highest standing in the village.

Not long after I entered school World War I broke out in Europe. The newspapers carried reports of the advance and retreat of the battle lines. The German Kaiser Wilhelm II had propounded the theory of a "yellow peril" threatening Europe and all of Christendom. In those days, though, we felt threatened by invasion from the West. There were rumors that the Germans were on their way from Berlin through Byzantium and Baghdad to attack Japan. That was the German 3B Plan. What we would do in case of German invasion was the object of lively debate among youngsters. We also discussed the 3A Plan. America would advance through Alaska and the Aleutian Islands, moving down from one island to the next until its armies pushed their way into Japan. To our young minds that too was an alarming thought.

When I was in the sixth grade, we went on a class trip to Yokohama, Kamakura, and Enoshima. This was the first time that I had ever been out of Yamanashi Prefecture, and the trip made a deep impression on me because everything seemed new and exciting. On a wharf in Yokohama a foreign woman slid her hand along the top of her handbag and it opened; she slid her hand back again and it closed—just like magic. I couldn't believe my eyes. I had never seen a zipper before.

I saw the ocean for the very first time in Kamakura. I had never seen the horizon stretch so far away. I couldn't help feeling that at any moment the ocean would roll in and swallow up the dry land in a single gulp.

SELF-EDUCATION

After six years of elementary school I could not ask my parents to support me any longer. When the final term came to an end I thought I would have to leave Hatsukari and go to work. My eldest brother had died in infancy, and my second- and third-eldest brothers had gone to Tokyo when they finished elementary school. Now it was my turn. What should I do? My parents said nothing. As young as I was, I gave serious thought to my future. In those days calligraphy by Ippei Wakao and Keijiro Amamiya were displayed in most of the houses in Hatsukari, probably because both these successful Yamanashi businessmen had started out as peddlers wearing straw sandals and carrying burdens dangling from poles across their backs. We had a framed work of calligraphy by Ippei Wakao at our house. These local success stories made a deep impression on me even as a young child. Yet I felt uneasy about starting out in life with only an elementary school education. Finally I talked it over with my parents and received their permission to take a two-year, upper-level course offered by my elementary school.

The classroom for the upper-level course was right next door to the elementary school. It was a one-room school shared by both first- and second-year students. The teachers were the same ones I had had in elementary school and the coursework was an extension of what I had studied there, with no classes in English or algebra. I subscribed to the National Middle School correspondence course and studied English, algebra, and geometry on my own. My English textbooks were transcribed into Japanese syllabics, and I learned the language by reading out loud sentences like "Itto izu a doggu." I still speak English with an accent.

I was very lucky. Takanori Kobayashi, who was a few years older than me, was studying for the entrance examination to the higher normal school. He had been born two doors down from my house and used to take time from his own studies to act as a substitute teacher. He was a very farsighted and ambitious young man, as the fact that he had finished middle school and was about to enter the higher normal school indicates. Hatsukari was a small town where there were no incentives whatsoever for young people to go on to higher education. Nevertheless I followed his advice and persevered with my studies.

Takanori was also a poet of the Araragi School, named after one of the leading poetry magazines of the day. Unfortunately he died young before he was able to achieve any of his ambitions. If I had had the inclination, perhaps I too might have learned to write *tanka* (poems of thirty-one syllables), but I threw myself into my studies instead and missed a unique opportunity.

Listening to Takanori Kobayashi, I realized what a tremendous effort would be required of me. The main problem was that I had grown up in a closed society surrounded on all sides by mountains, and I knew nothing of the outside world. But everyone will work hard if only there is an incentive to do so. This was something I discovered early, and it continued to be my philosophy years later when I led NEC into the world market.

The more I studied the National Middle School correspondence course, the more interesting my studies became. I can do this, I told myself. I will go on to middle school. Three or four of my former classmates were already in middle school, however, and there was no way that I was going to be put into a lower grade than they were in. I asked the middle school authorities to allow me to enter as a third-year student. They said I could if I passed a special examination. Needless to say I got my parents' permission and took the test.

The big hurdle was the examination in English conversation. The English teacher, Mr. Seijiro Ogiwara, asked, "How old are you?" After studying English in Japanese syllabics, I was thoroughly disconcerted to hear him speaking the language fluently. I lost my composure and blurted out, "I am fifty years old." *"Fifty?"* I'm done for, I thought, and quickly corrected myself. *"Fifteen,"* I said. Certain that I had failed, I returned home with a heavy heart. But the next day I received notice that I had passed. Had the examiner taken pity on me?

On the first day of school I was hauled before the school bullies. They made me sit in the lecture hall while they berated me for having the presumption to enter middle school at the third-year level. I was sure they were going to beat me up, but fortunately they didn't. I had passed yet another test successfully.

Matsumoto High School

Tsuru Middle School, which I entered in 1921 as a third-year student, was five miles away from my home. Although there was a train, I walked there and back every day in order to save the train fare. Shoes were too expensive to walk in, so I kept them at school for sports and wore wooden clogs instead.

Every day in wind and rain I made that ten-mile round trip. It took four hours, and by the time I returned home I was so exhausted I couldn't study. Instead I studied as I walked. Walking made me hungry, so I kept dried slices of steamed sweet potato in my pockets and ate as I went along.

The former governor of Aichi Prefecture, Mikine Kuwabara, had been in the first graduating class of Tsuru Middle School. His achievements were legendary. He was said to have walked twelve miles a day to and from school. It was like that in those days.

My mother would wake up every morning at half past four and make a lunch for me. She must have had a very hard life. Even now, I get a lump in my throat whenever I think of her. She overcame innumerable difficulties and continued to look after our home in the countryside until she died at the age of eighty-three. In August 1987 services commemorating the thirty-third anniversary of her death were held back home in Hatsukari.

After I entered the middle school, I learned about the school's scholarship system. Anyone who maintained an average of ninety or above in his coursework was exempted from paying tuition. I decided to study hard in order to qualify for the exemption. My grade average as a third-year student was ninety-four. My hopes were duly fulfilled when I became a scholarship student the next year. My parents were extremely pleased for me.

The teachers at middle school who made the greatest impression on me were my physics teacher, Mr. Usaburo Ogiwara, and my Chinese classics teacher, Mr. Akiyori Hojo. Mr. Hojo was very strict but very kindhearted; he seemed to embody the Confucian ethics that he taught. Many years later I was again made aware of his extraordinary thoughtfulness.

I had vaguely supposed that when I graduated from middle school I would go off to Tokyo to work. But gradually it dawned on me that even at a country school like Tsuru Middle School, fourth-year students could prepare to take the entrance examinations and go on for higher education. Beyond middle school was high school—under the prewar system high schools were more like colleges than like the high schools of today—and beyond high school was university. Each year two or three boys from my middle school went on to high school. But there was almost no incentive to do so, consequently my fellow students were an unambitious lot who scarcely seemed to know that high schools or universities existed.

I began to see getting into high school as my one-way ticket out of the countryside and rose to the challenge. But how would I pay the tuition? That was an enormous problem, but I decided to postpone worrying about it until after I had been admitted and to concentrate on passing the entrance exam. Which high school should I apply to—the Number One High School, in Tokyo, or Matsumoto High, where I had a better chance of being accepted? I had heard that only incredible geniuses went to the Number One High School; Matsumoto High would be easier, so I decided to apply there. Once I was accepted, tuition became my major concern. In those days there were very few scholarships and no such thing as part-time jobs for those wanting to work their way through school. There seemed to be no other way but to ask my parents for the money—but I didn't feel I could ask them for any more help. Convinced that I had to resolve the problem on my own, I turned to my older brothers and asked them for a loan so I could at least begin the school semester. Once all the arrangements were complete, I left home and headed for Matsumoto.

My father came with me to the matriculation ceremonies. As a present he had bought me a brand-new cap. I put it on and was about to join my new classmates when I looked around and saw that the caps they were all wearing were old and tattered. None of them had a shining new one like mine. Embarrassed, I scuffed it up so that it would look like everyone else's and put it back on. A bandanna flapping at the hips, wooden clogs on the feet—the rough-and-ready look was the height of fashion then, and there was a stigma attached to anyone who didn't follow the trend. My father looked on and didn't say a word.

That evening I got my first taste of life in a dormitory. A party for incoming students was held in the cafeteria. At the entrance was an enormous open cask of clear liquid. We were supposed to dip our teacups in it and gulp it down. Though it was cold sake, it looked just like water and I drank one cup of it after another. There were also cigarettes lying around the room. I had never smoked or drunk alcohol before, and to do both at the same time proved too much for me. That night I was so sick I was sure I would die. I learned my lesson, though, and for the next three years of high school I hardly touched alcohol and cigarettes again.

The city of Matsumoto in Nagano Prefecture is famous for its location in the Japan Alps. My professors used to urge us to look up and enjoy the beautiful scenery. But it didn't seem particularly special to me; after all, I had been born and bred in Hatsukari, a village surrounded by mountains.

ONE-UPMANSHIP

Once I had gotten into Matsumoto High School, my most pressing concern once again was how to raise the money for tuition. Surely, someone somewhere would provide tuition for me. And so I began to search for a benefactor. When I consulted with the student advisor, I learned that an inquiry had come from the Nomura Scholarship Society. "Tokushichi Nomura of Osaka says that he will pay your tuition if you pass the examination. Is that agreeable?" I immediately asked the advisor to write a letter of introduction for me and set off for Osaka.

I had never heard of Tokushichi Nomura, who later went on to found the Nomura Securities Company. He must have been around forty then. I told him I didn't have enough money to pay for tuition and asked for his support. "All right," he said, "I will support you. I don't want the money back. Just be sure to study hard so that you can go out and make the world a better place." I was deeply moved. With youthful idealism I resolved anew to work hard and make a contribution to the world and to humanity.

During the summer vacation of 1923, the year I entered high school, I returned home to Hatsukari. On September 1, I was preparing for my second semester, when the Great Kanto Earthquake struck. It was just noon. I rushed out of the house and grabbed hold of a persimmon tree in the garden to prop myself up. I was sure that at any moment the earth would split open.

The persimmon tree is still standing beside the house where I was born.

There were four classes at Matsumoto High School: Science A and B and Liberal Arts A and B. In my class, Science A, was a mathematical genius from Matsumoto Middle School named Tosaku Mizuhashi. Mathematics was very advanced at Matsumoto Middle School. Fourth-year students there had already finished differential calculus, which students in my middle school didn't take until the fifth year.

But I have never been the type that likes to be beaten. I studied like mad and challenged Mizuhashi to a one-on-one test of skill. Which of us could hand in his examination papers faster?

All our classmates looked on with deep interest. I won once. It was a two-hour exam, but I finished it in thirty minutes. Now came the climactic moment. If I checked my answers, Mizuhashi would pass his test paper in ahead of me. I called the teacher over and asked with my eyes if my answers were correct. He nodded yes, and needless to say, I got my test in first. I can still remember Mizuhashi's chagrin.

Because I was in the science course, naturally I concentrated most of my efforts on the sciences. But I once made the nearly catastrophic mistake of not taking my nonscience subjects seriously enough. Before the final examination in the first term of my law and economics course, the professor told us that the exam questions were a matter of common sense, so there was no need to prepare. I took him at his word and, relying upon my common sense to write the exam, failed spectacularly. A failure in one subject meant that you could not go on to the next grade. During the second and third terms I studied as one possessed to pass the course. What was common sense to a professor and common sense to a young man from deep in the mountains was as different as night and day.

But I also had the opposite experience. When I was a second-year student my psychology professor announced that someone had received a perfect score. I remember wondering who it could have been—only to discover it was me.

I also remember a curious occasion when I saved one of my classmates from missing a test. Since the seating plan was in the order of the Japanese syllabary, my friend K always sat on my right and we were in the same room in the dormitory. During one exam I looked to my right and noticed that K was not there. That seemed very strange since I knew he had been studying far into the night. I raised my hand and said to the professor, "Please don't pass the exam out yet. K studied very hard for this test, but he isn't here. Something must have happened to him. Let me go and find out." I raced over to the dorm and found K sound asleep in the closet. Exhausted from studying all night he had curled up there at dawn and gone to sleep. I woke him up and dragged him over to the examination hall, where fortunately, our professor had waited for us. The pace of life was slower in those days.

Memories of my science courses, which I had a natural aptitude for, come flooding back to me. But not all those memories are good ones. I remember that the chemistry lectures were delivered so rapidly I couldn't take notes. And I could hardly endure the smell of hydrogen sulfide in our chemistry experiments. But my physics professor, Mr. Fujimura, taught us very thoroughly, making eye contact with each of us as he lectured.

Because I liked math and physics, it seemed only natural that I would go to university and study electrical engineering. The entrance examination for electrical engineering at that time was the hardest one of all. I immediately rose to the challenge with never a thought about what I would do if I failed. In order to prepare for the examination, I took lodgings during my third year. The first room I lived in was above a grocery store. At the tobacco shop across the way lived a pretty girl who was related to the owner of the grocery store. When she occasionally brought meals up to my room, I was so shy I couldn't even raise my head to look at her.

ELECTRICAL ENGINEERING AT TOKYO IMPERIAL UNIVERSITY

When the time came I unhesitatingly selected the Department of Electrical Engineering in the School of Engineering at Tokyo Imperial University, the most exacting of all Japanese universities. Knowing that if I failed I would have to try something else,

I staked my entire future on that single examination. But I have always believed that when pressed to make a choice we should never think of failure, only of doing our best. How we handle the challenges we face is the yardstick by which we must measure our lives. Fortunately I was accepted into Tokyo University and entered its gates in April 1926.

Unlike in middle or high school, the relationship between university professors and their students was a very close one. I remember Professor Matsujiro Oyama's course on electro-magnetism and electrothermal engineering; Professor Shoji Seto on electrical machinery engineering; Professor Motoji Shibusawa on engineering for power stations and transmission; Professor Ken Nishi on high-voltage engineering; Professor Tsunetaro Ku-jirai on radio-wave engineering; Associate Professor Yoshikazu Omoto on illumination engineering; Associate Professor Masa-haru Hoshiai on electrical measurements; and Associate Professor Hideo Yamashita on electrical testing methods.

Listing my professors and coursework in this way makes it sound as though I did nothing but study. But in fact I enjoyed myself, rowing on the Sumida River, which runs through the eastern side of downtown Tokyo, and taking part in other pas-times. Some of my classmates played *shogi* and *go*, both Japanese board games, but I was not one of them. I had no aptitude whatsoever for such games. When I was at Tsuru Middle School my brother Teiji, five years my junior, would always beat me.

Teiji was a brilliant student, who had finished the five-year course at Tsuru Middle School in four years and had gone on to the Liberal Arts A Class at Number One High School, in Tokyo. He belonged to the school debating club and for no apparent reason was forced to leave school on ideological grounds. Those were bad times. Teiji became ill and returned to Hatsukari to recuperate. At every possible opportunity, however, he was sum-moned before the local police. He died in June 1935, at the age of twenty-three. My father followed him a year later, dying in July 1936 when he was sixty-nine. I always felt that anxiety over my brother had caused my father's death.

When I was a second-year student we translated and published the collected works of Charles P. Steinmetz, the foremost au-thority on electrical engineering of the day. Shigenari Miyamoto and Toshifusa Sakamoto were in charge of the project, and I was a member of the translation team. I worked hard on that translation and for my share of the work was paid one hundred yen— the monthly entry-level salary for a college graduate. I remember receiving the money from the Corona Publishing Company, putting my wallet in the pocket of my overcoat, and boarding the streetcar. On the way home I realized someone had picked my pocket, but by then it was too late. What a bitter disappointment! I have never been able to forget it.

For three months during my final year at the university, from September to December 1928, I lived in Nagano Prefecture at the foot of the Japan Alps, as a trainee at a power station being constructed at Yukawato on the Azusa River. Three of my classmates were also trainees at the Nagawato power station nearby. As autumn advanced the mountains were tinged with red foliage. Kamikochi, a popular mountain resort, was not far away and occasionally we would walk there. One day, to our great surprise, we met a bear on the way.

During our internship our senior coworkers invited some of their female relations and held a party in our honor to thank us for our services. At that party I touched the hand of a young girl for the first time. A shock raced through my body like an electric current. I was still almost embarrassingly naive.

When the training period was over I had to write up a report and submit my thesis, which was on remote supervisory control systems, a subject that I had been thinking about for some time. Once my trainee's report had been judged satisfactory and I had finished my thesis, the time came to decide upon a place of employment.

2

MY EARLY YEARS
AT NEC

ASSIGNED TO THE
ENGINEERING SECTION

The foremost researcher in the area of remote supervisory control systems, the topic of my thesis, was Yasujiro Shimazu, an engineer at Nippon Electric Company. I therefore tentatively decided on NEC as my first choice for employment. When I made this decision known to Professor Oyama, my placement advisor, he was less than enthusiastic. "NEC is a subsidiary of Western Electric in the U.S.," he said. "I don't think it will suit you to work for a foreign-controlled company." Despite his words of warning, I chose NEC.

I had an interview with Genichiro Ohata, the managing director at NEC. Joining the company with me at the same time were Yuji Uchida, a graduate of Kyoto University, and Ryozo Suzuki of Hokkaido University. At last I was about to become a full-fledged member of society. On April 1, 1929, I entered NEC and was assigned to the Engineering Section. On April 15 I was told to attend an installation of our machinery at the Electrotechnical Laboratory of the Ministry of Communications. Although I had diligently studied the blueprints for these machines, I had never seen the real things before. I didn't have a clue about what was going on. As soon as I left, the head of the laboratory got on the phone and asked, "Who was that fellow who came in today? He doesn't know a thing."

For my part, I kept thinking this wasn't why I'd come to NEC. I was there to do research. But the Great Depression was just beginning, so there was nothing at the company to do. Of the fifteen hundred employees at NEC half were factory workers, but they had almost no work. Office employees were told, "Don't waste paper. Don't turn on the lights." Finally International Standard Electric Corporation, the subsidiary of International Telephone and Telegraph that was in charge of managing NEC, couldn't stand the situation any longer and transferred the management rights to the Sumitomo Honsha Company in 1932.

Despite these management difficulties, the engineers at NEC were kept busy. In October of 1929, I was ordered to go to Kyushu to make repairs to remote supervisory control equipment at National Railways that was not functioning properly. I set off for Kyushu, traveling from station to station by trolley car between the regularly scheduled train service. I soon realized what the problem was: the station attendants had twisted the relay contacts needed for fine tuning with a pair of pliers. No wonder the control system didn't work. I traveled the entire line of National Railways in Kyushu showing the workers how to make the necessary adjustments. The people at National Railways must have felt grateful for my efforts, because they invited me to a spa in Oita Prefecture and held a party in my honor. The combination of exhaustion and alcohol proved too much for me, however, and I got thoroughly drunk.

In 1930 I did my compulsory service in the Japanese Army as a military cadet in the Nakano Telegraph Corps. In the telegraph corps we had to know how to ride, but I was no good with horses. Being intelligent creatures, the horses seemed to sense this and were not willing to comply when I tried to mount. It was quite an ordeal. Finally, in the autumn of 1930, after a ten-month tour of duty, I received my discharge from military service. The following year the Manchurian Incident occurred, and Manchuria (now the northeastern sector of the People's Republic of China) came under Japanese control.

After I returned to NEC I suddenly became very busy. Work was beginning in earnest on the South Manchuria Railway, and a multiplex carrier telephone system had to be installed along the train lines. Tomotsuchi Ushida, who had been in the class ahead of me at Tokyo Imperial University and had entered the company the year before I did, was in charge of the project.

Shimazu's remote supervisory control system and the phototelegraph equipment developed by Chief Engineer Yasujiro Niwa were the only two technological breakthroughs made by NEC itself; otherwise almost all the communications equipment was based on Western Electric technology. We young engineers were far from happy with this situation. Ushida wanted to enlarge the three-channel carrier telephone system developed by Western into a four-channel system, but his supervisor was against the idea. "It is risky to try something Western hasn't already done," he was told. When Ushida heard this he decided that it was hopeless to work at NEC any longer and left to get a job with a competitor, Toyo Communication Equipment, where he could develop the system he had devised.

Before he left he called me in and said, "I know you are dissatisfied too with the way the company is being run. Why don't you come with me? I will be chief engineer and make twice my present salary. You could be assistant chief engineer and make half as much again as you do now. How about it?" It was true that I was dissatisfied with NEC and any proposal that involved a raise in salary could not be rejected lightly. "Give me a night to think it over," I said. The next day I gave him my answer: "I'm sorry but I am staying with NEC—although I intend to reform the company from top to bottom."

Toyo Communication Equipment is now an affiliate of NEC. How strange the way things work out.

The Power-Line Carrier
Telephone System

In 1934 the power-line carrier telephone that I had developed was the lead story on the human interest page of the *Jiji Shinpo* newspaper. This system utilized electric power transmission lines for telephone use. The idea itself was not new; indeed, the system is said to have been originally invented in Japan in 1919 at the Electrotechnical Laboratory of the Ministry of Communications.

NEC commenced development of the power-line carrier telephone around 1933. At the time only General Electric in the United States and Siemens in Germany were producing such equipment. But after investigating the matter I discovered that the products of both these companies were based on electric power technology. For that reason NEC decided to develop an alternative system based on communications technology.

A Tokyo University classmate of mine, Shigenari Miyamoto, was doing work in electric power at the Shibaura Engineering Works (now the Toshiba Corporation). This friendship of ours led to cooperation between our two companies on the power-line carrier telephone project. In 1934 our experiments met with success. We used the power transmission lines between the Nippon Electric Power Company's Yanagawara power station in Toyama Prefecture and the Tokyo Electric Light Company's transmission substation at Tsurumi near Tokyo. Jiro Higuchi, a graduate of the Tokyo Institute of Technology who had just entered NEC, worked with me and was of great assistance.

Now we needed to sell the idea to an electric power company. Since my supervisors seemed at a loss as to what to do, I proposed that we approach the Changjin River Hydroelectric Power Company in northern Korea. No one approved of my suggestion. In those days NEC was under the direct patronage of the Ministry of Communications and was quite weak at sales. I suppose my superiors were afraid it might cause embarrassment if we were to try to sell equipment that not even our parent company, Western Electric, had any experience with.

Since I could not turn to anyone else for assistance, I made an appointment myself with Shitagau Noguchi, the president of Changjin Hydro, and visited the company's head office in Tokyo. Noguchi, the founder of the Noguchi financial combine, was a farsighted man with visions of building a mammoth electric power company that would stretch from Korea into China. I had heard of these plans; in fact, that was why I was calling on him with my proposal. I also thought that only an engineer like myself could give an adequate explanation of the technology involved.

I still vividly remember our first conversation. I was a junior NEC employee only a few years out of school facing a captain of industry many years my senior who had graduated from the Electrical Engineering Department of Tokyo Imperial University in 1907, the year I was born. Mr. Noguchi was sitting with his feet up on his desk while I stood stiffly at attention. "Kobayashi, I graduated from Tokyo University in electrical engineering too, you know. This electric power-line carrier equipment of yours, I suppose it's simply a matter of flicking a switch here and it's on, turn a switch there and you're connected to the circuit." I wanted to say, "No, you're wrong." But I hung my head and said merely, "I've added a few refinements. Please use it for your company's communications between Seoul and Changjin River."

One day after my second or third visit he said, "How much?" When I said eighty thousand yen he shot back, "Siemens will sell it to me for fifty thousand." I returned to NEC, got the company to agree to fifty thousand and went back to Noguchi. Imagine my surprise when this time he said, "Siemens says it'll do it for thirty thousand." I was sure that I had lost and my shoulders sagged in disappointment. Immediately Noguchi's expression softened. "Since I feel sorry for you, I'll buy one model from Siemens and one from NEC." My power-line carrier telephone system was called the PL-1; it was my maiden effort.

Because a college classmate of mine, Tatsuo Monoi, used to work for Changjin Hydro, I heard from him often in later years. My equipment was still in operation right up to the time of the Korean War.

THE NONLOADED-CABLE CARRIER TELEPHONE SYSTEM

In the mid-1920s two young engineers at the Ministry of Communications were passionately dedicated to the idea of Japanese development of multiplex-cable carrier communications equipment. Their names were Shigeyoshi Matsumae, now the president of Tokai University, and the late Noboru Shinohara, a classmate of mine at Tokyo Imperial University. Matsumae had conceived of a carrier communications system using nonloaded cable, a new and unique communications method for the world at that time. What had been used until then was the loaded-cable method invented in the United States by Professor Michael I. Pupin. The problem with this method was that transmission distances were limited because of the delay time caused by loading coils inserted along the cable.

Matsumae and his staff had noticed the improvements that

were being made to high-gain vacuum-tube amplifiers and reasoned that the use of such amplifiers could compensate for the attenuation of a signal as it was being sent over the cables and could restore it to its original strength. At the time this was a revolutionary idea. If the method succeeded, not only would it be possible to build economical telephone circuits, but also transmission distances could be extended many times farther than was presently possible.

Fumio Shida, the managing director at NEC, had promised Matsumae the company's complete support, and that was how I became involved in the development of the nonloaded-cable carrier telephone system. My assistants were Yujiro Degawa, who had graduated from the Tokyo Institute of Technology in 1933 and served as Professor Isamu Yamamoto's assistant there before joining NEC, and Takeo Kurokawa, who had entered NEC upon graduation from Kyoto University in 1937.

In 1934 we had tried an experiment using submarine telegraph cables as part of a telephone circuit linking Yoshimi in Yamaguchi Prefecture with Pusan in Korea. The cables had been installed by a Dutch company around 1910. We used an amplifier to magnify the sound of the voice and conducted the experiment in the middle of the night when it was most likely to be quiet. I was at Pusan, and when I heard the faint sound of a voice speaking to me from Yoshimi on the Japanese side, I was so excited that my eyes filled with tears.

This experiment bore fruit in March 1937 in the three-channel nonloaded-cable circuit between Andong (now Dandong) and Mukden (now Shenyang in the People's Republic of China). The circuits were used by the newly founded Manchurian Telegraph and Telephone Company (MTT). Another Tokyo University classmate of mine, Shinji Shiota, worked for MTT. In 1939 a 1,875-mile nonloaded-cable carrier telephone circuit—the longest in the world—was completed between Tokyo and Mukden. As the person in charge of this project for NEC, I made frequent visits to Manchuria. Trains on the South Manchuria Railway were frequently attacked by bands of insurgents. In the hills around the construction sites we could often see their bonfires at night and did not dare to go out of the relay stations that were then being built. One time while Shinohara was on an inspection tour, the rebels attacked, and his military escort had to fight them off.

My increasing business trips to Manchuria resulted in a turning point in my life quite unrelated to my work. At Port Arthur (Lüshun in the People's Republic of China) there was an engineering college that I often visited on business. Its president was Seiichiro Noda, a graduate of the Electrical Department of Kyoto University, who had been an associate professor there and had subsequently studied at Cornell University in the United States. After teaching at the Kumamoto Higher Engineering School (now Kumamoto University), he had become president of the Lüshun Institute of Technology. His specialty was electrical mathematics, and he was said to have been the first in Japan to introduce matrix theory into electrical engineering.

Chance relationships are very mysterious. While visiting Port Arthur I became acquainted with Professor Noda's eldest daughter, Kazuko, who had returned home to Port Arthur after graduating from the Shoin Women's College in Osaka. Kazuko and I were married in Tokyo at Alumni Hall on March 10, 1935. Shigeyoshi Matsumae and Professor Takashi Otsuki of the Tokyo Institute of Technology, who had taught with Professor Noda in Kumamoto, had consented to act as our go-betweens.

All too often, after having been under pressure for a long time, one's health disintegrates as soon as there is a breathing space. Shortly after the wedding I began to run a low-grade fever. I had been seriously ill before, in 1932. Then, trying to meet a deadline for the delivery of new products, I had stayed up three nights in a row. When I became feverish I stuck my feet in a bucket of cold water and kept on working. Such determination proved my undoing. On my way home I stopped in at a clinic in the Shinjuku district of Tokyo. The doctor who examined me said I was seriously ill with pleurisy; my chest was filled with fluid. He prescribed complete bed rest, and the next day I went into the hospital. After three months under medical care I would know immediately whenever my temperature went up as little as one-half of a degree.

Right after my marriage I suppose I must have complained about not feeling well. Saburo Akaza, who worked in my laboratory, told me not to work so hard and suggested I take up astronomy. He even lent me his telescope. I found it very soothing to gaze up at the heavens every night. I was particularly fascinated by the planet Saturn with its seven colored rings. Looking at it I was overwhelmed by the mystery of the universe. In two or three months my health returned to normal.

Once I had regained my health I started to write my doctoral dissertation. Just about that time Managing Director Shida made the very welcome suggestion that I go abroad on a study tour. Although I had not completed my thesis, I could hardly ask him to put off the trip until the thesis was finished. Instead I used the pressure of work as an excuse and got an extension from Tokyo University. I handed in my thesis in November 1937. It was entitled "A Study of the Negative-Feedback Amplifier."

THE DOMESTIC PRODUCTION MOVEMENT

It is interesting to look back to the early days of communications technology in Japan. The person who made the most impact in this field was without question Shigeyoshi Matsumae of the Ministry of Communications. He had insisted that the nonloaded-cable carrier telephone had to be developed without resorting to foreign-held patents, and this fact was expressly stated in the ministry's specification sheet.

Out of curiosity my colleagues and I checked through various patents only to discover that foreign patents were held even on what seemed to us matters of common sense. Take the case of the negative-feedback amplifier. This had been invented by an engineer at the Bell Laboratories in the U.S., which naturally enough held the patent for it. But surprisingly a European company, though later than Bell in submitting its patent application, held a wider range of patents on the feedback amplifier than Bell did. Because the negative-feedback amplifier was a very important topic in my own research, the patent situation was something I could not afford to ignore.

Having conceived the idea for a multiplex-feedback amplifier, I applied for a generalized patent on feedback amplifiers, fully expecting foreign companies to lodge an objection. My strategy would be to invite their objections, if any, and call their attention to the original ideas embodied in my patent application. But there were no statements of protest. My strategy had misfired, and instead NEC held a wide-ranging patent on feedback amplifiers. I had no intention of using our patent rights to exclude other companies, but only to protect NEC's interests. My technical accounts of this patent appeared in Japanese in the *Journal of the Institute of Electrical Communication Engineers.*

Through this incident I learned the importance of patents and used to urge my colleagues at NEC to apply for as many as possible. I myself submitted approximately five applications a month and within four years had applied for more than one hundred patents or utility models, most of which were duly registered at the Patent Office. For one of these, the feedback compandor, I received a medal from the Imperial Invention Association of Japan.

I have another memory of Shigeyoshi Matsumae, of quite a different sort. Matsumae came back from a tour of Denmark full of enthusiasm for Danish gymnastics. The people of Denmark woke up every morning and did these exercises, he reported, and Japan should too. He founded the Bosei Gakujuku Institute, otherwise known as the Matsumae School, and I became a student there, attending several times a month. Danish gymnastics were very good, but the vault absolutely defeated me. In those days I weighed over 180 pounds and was quite plump; nevertheless, I was supposed to put my hands on the vault, do a handstand, then flip over and land on my feet on the other side. Only two people couldn't master the vault, Noboru Shinohara and I. Matsumae goaded me on, saying I couldn't do it because I didn't have the nerve, until I became so furious I didn't care what happened. I simply leaped up, somersaulted over the vault, and sprained my ankle. The next day I left for Manchuria on crutches with a compress around my leg. Matsumae had given me quite a workout, but I bore him no ill will.

A BUSINESS TRIP ABROAD

In December 1937 NEC sent me on a study tour abroad, and I set sail from Yokohama on the *Chichibu-maru* bound for the United States. Life aboard ship was completely Western-style. Etiquette for dinner was particularly punctilious. Every evening before dinner I bathed, put on a black suit, and went to the dining room. The menu was so sumptuous that later, during the war when I had nothing to eat, I would often dream about those meals. After dinner there was dancing, but since I couldn't dance I would sit along the wall and watch.

As soon as I arrived in New York I went to see Harold S. Black, the inventor of the negative-feedback amplifier, at the Bell Laboratories. Bell had arranged for me to meet Black in the presence of the chief of their licensing department. Perhaps they were being cautious because they knew that I was doing research in the same area. I came straight to the point and asked Black what had given him the idea for his negative-feedback amplifier. "We have a great mathematician by the name of Harry Nyquist in our laboratories," he replied. "I left the theoretical investigation of my ideas up to him. Actually those ideas were related to his regeneration theory, so you might say that teamwork led to the birth of this new amplifier." When I heard Black's explanation I was thunderstruck. That sort of interdisciplinary approach was just what one would expect from a great research institution like Bell Laboratories, and I understood how it could facilitate such revolutionary invention.

Many years later at a conference in Boston in 1961, the Institute of Electrical and Electronics Engineers (IEEE) awarded Dr. Nyquist their Medal of Honor for his outstanding achievements in engineering science and technology. In his address Nyquist grumbled that "scientific papers nowadays contain nothing but difficult formulae so I can barely understand them." Everyone there burst out laughing. No doubt they all felt relieved to hear such complaints coming from the master of difficult theories himself.

My tour of a New York telephone office also left a strong impression on me. The supervisor there, a woman, told me with unshakable confidence that one day it would be possible to make telephone connections to anywhere in the country in less than three minutes. I was amazed. In Japan the telephone was still in its infancy. To reach the NEC head office in Mita from the plant where I worked in Kawasaki City, it took one hour by automobile, two hours by electric train, and half a day by telephone. To put a telephone call through to Osaka from Tokyo—a distance of about three hundred miles—took a whole day.

Although I had entered NEC, a company that produced telephones, in 1929, it was not until after the war that I had a telephone installed in my own home. I couldn't afford it, and since none of my colleagues had a telephone either, there seemed no point in having one. I finally got a telephone at home in 1946, thanks to a conversation with a company messenger boy. When I became head of the plant at Tamagawa, this messenger was constantly carrying memos from the head office to my home in Himonya. One day he said to me, "Since our company makes telephones, why don't you have one installed?" "I can't afford it," I told him bluntly. "And I don't think it would be worthwhile. I know it's hard on you having to come out here all the time on company business, and if the company installed one here, I wouldn't object." No doubt he was delighted to hear this, because he immediately informed someone in the head office. That was how, after working seventeen years for a company that manufactured communications equipment, I finally got a telephone in my own home at company expense.

After finishing my tour of the United States I headed for Europe on the luxury liner *Queen Mary*. Life on board ship was very pleasant. In Europe I visited the central laboratories of Siemens in Germany in order to meet Dr. Hans Ferdinand Mayer. He and Shigeyoshi Matsumae had had a major dispute over Matsumae's proposal for a nonloaded-cable system. In 1933, when Matsumae had been visiting Europe, he had written to a colleague in the Ministry of Communications about his argument with Mayer, so I had very much wanted to meet the man. We arranged a time for the meeting, but the taxi driver got lost and I was thirty minutes late. As soon as Mayer saw me, he stormed out of the room in a rage. "You kept me waiting thirty minutes," he said. "So I'll keep you waiting thirty minutes." Mayer was a typical German gentleman with a dueling scar on his cheek. As Matsumae had done I contended that a nonloaded-cable system was the superior method, but Mayer would not concede and insisted that a very lightly loaded cable system was better. Although we disagreed, it was an interesting experience.

Originally I had planned to board ship at Marseilles and sail directly home, but instead I sailed back to America on the *Queen Mary* to visit the U.S. Bureau of Standards and other places that my schedule had prevented me from going to earlier. My company had given me permission to travel abroad for one year, but because of exchange restrictions I was able to bring only a limited amount of money with me. The result was that no matter how I did my calculations, I had enough money for only eight months. I had just come to the end of my finances, when quite by accident I met a senior colleague, Masatsugu Kobayashi, who had just arrived in New York from Tokyo. He was truly a friend in need. "This is very difficult to ask you," I said, "but I've run out of money. Could you lend me a hundred dollars?" Kobayashi kindly complied. I sailed from Seattle on the *Hikawa-maru*. When I landed in Yokohama, I spent the last of my money on a tip to the porter. It took me a whole year to pay Kobayashi back.

I have sad memories of Managing Director Shida, who had given me permission to go abroad. While I was in southern Europe I received word of his death. I could hardly believe it. He had been on his way back from a business trip to Manchuria when he died suddenly of acute pneumonia. Shortly after I landed in Yokohama I visited Mr. Shida's home to pay my respects. Mr. Shida's father, Rinsaburo Shida, had been a pioneer in electrical engineering who had received an engineering doctorate during the early Meiji period (1868–1912). Mr. Shida himself had graduated from the School of Engineering at Kyoto University and had been a student when my father-in-law was teaching there. My father-in-law had known him well.

QUELLING LABOR UNREST

After my year abroad the nature of my work changed completely. The day after my return I received the official notification of my appointment as assistant manager of the Special Products Section. I was put in charge of work related to underwater weaponry for the Japanese Navy. My superior was Captain Mori, but a short time later, when he left to become a high-level advisor to the company, I was promoted and given responsibility for the entire navy plant.

My first task was to create an efficient organization and make the most appropriate use of the staff at my disposal. I started to study management and personnel systems. When my study showed results, I began to grow interested in management. My efforts to organize the office staff went so smoothly that I decided to try my hand at reorganizing the factory workers. The managers and supervisors at the plant had never tried to interfere with the workers before. But I, with no experience outside of research and development, was unaware of that fact. I plunged ahead and replaced the powerful labor boss of the factory with an up-and-coming younger worker.

When I arrived at work the morning after the official announcement of this change, the plant was on strike. The workers were clustered together in groups of threes and fours, holding whispered conversations. Although we were right in the middle of the war in China, the workers were sabotaging the plant. The situation was serious. I wondered if I had gone a bit too far, and sent out agents to find out what was happening. From them I learned that the powerful labor boss had issued an order to sabotage work at the plant.

I had no alternative but to meet with the man and listen to what he had to say, so I called him into my office. I had heard that he carried a dagger, and because everyone was afraid, no one dared criticize him. Some sort of compromise seemed in order. "Being new on the job I had no idea what an important person you are," I told him. "Won't you become factory foreman?" "I'm not the type to become foreman," he replied. "I choose the foreman around here—not you." I called him in the next day and asked him to reconsider. Again he refused. "If you try anything," he threatened, "I'll quit and take all the experienced workers with me and shut this plant down."

With the war going on in China the company needed its skilled workers more than ever before. I could not tell the head office what was going on, so I had to come up with a solution by myself. That night I decided to visit the homes of the most influential and experienced workers. Because of the blackout the houses were in total darkness as I went from door to door telling the whole story to the wives and appealing for their help. "Your husband has perhaps said something to you about quitting. Please don't let him. There is a troublemaker who is leading him on. Please persuade him to stay." The wives were clearly surprised, but my plan worked.

Two or three days later I had won. I told the head of Personnel that I was firing the labor boss. "Give him a letter of recommendation so he can find a job at another firm at twenty to thirty percent more than his current income." Then I called him in again and told him he was fired. After things had calmed down, the efficiency rating at the plant rose markedly. Needless to say, my showdown with the agitator stood me in good stead later in my management career.

As the war expanded, so did the scope of our operations, and we became involved not merely with production but with the research and development of new weapons. I put an engineer named Chosuke Sugi in charge of developing a magnetic torpedo. I presented a plan based on his ideas to the navy. A magnetic torpedo consists of an electric wire wound around a magnetic core. When the device approaches an area where there are changes in the magnetic field, a fuse is activated and the device explodes. The device works provided the wire is wound between one and two hundred thousand times, but navy authorities demanded we decrease that number and refused to use the weapon until we did. Some time later we were able to get our hands on a U.S.-made magnetic torpedo that had been used at Guadalcanal, a simple device wound no more than one hundred thousand times or so. But the Japanese Navy would not use a weapon unless it was infallible. Could anything be more bureaucratic and unscientific? Everything is a matter of degree. Because the navy refused to understand this, the U.S. got ahead of us with the magnetic torpedo.

Becoming Plant Manager

The Special Products Section that I headed was upgraded to an Underwater Acoustic Products Plant, which made a wide range of secret weapons for the navy, including underwater sonar and sound detectors. In 1943 I was promoted to plant manager. One year later in 1944 we were hit by a labor shortage. Middle school students from Kawasaki City were mobilized to work at the plant.

My heart went out to those poor innocent children as they

worked drenched in sweat for the sake of their country. But there are evil people in this world. Some bullies among the draftees were preying on these innocent children and stealing their money. Teachers from the middle school came and complained that as plant manager it was my responsibility to do something. Here we were in the middle of a world war with our country's fate in the balance. I could hardly suppress my indignation at what was happening.

I immediately looked into the situation and discovered there were about ten bullies in all, one of whom lorded it over the others. This man had been a house painter before he was drafted, and his entire body was covered with tattoos just like a gangster. Every day around noon he would bring out a washtub, put it in the middle of the plant, strip to his loincloth, and wash himself. Whether they wanted to or not, the other workers were obliged to watch this daily exhibition of his tattoos, but they were too afraid of him to complain. I checked out the place where the bully took his tub bath. Somehow I would have to put him in his place. One day I made up my mind. I would make a tour of the plant at the very time he was taking his bath.

I stood at the entrance to the plant and looked in: the man with the tattoos was just beginning to bathe. For a moment I didn't want to go through with it, but I plucked up my courage and walked in. All the workers, including the section chiefs and group leaders, stood tensely by, pretending not to see what was happening. I had gone too far to pull back now. I walked straight up to the man and said, "Your behavior is unforgivable." I gave him a shove and sent him staggering. I must have caught him by surprise because he just stood there dumbfounded. To avoid any further trouble I quickly returned to my office. I knew more or less who the other nine thugs were, so I contacted them through the head of Personnel and called them one by one into the room. As an officer in the local military reserve unit, I always kept a sword in the office. I drew it out, laid it against the cheek of each of the bullies, and began to speak: "I suppose you carry a dagger. How about fighting with a real sword? I'm not going to let you get away with extorting pocket money from children." They all turned pale and promised never to do it again. The problem was solved.

After that incident the ringleader began to go around saying,

"Mr. Kobayashi is my boss." When labor disputes began to get violent after the war, he used to walk close beside me and say over and over again, "Anybody who tries to lay a hand on Mr. Kobayashi will have to answer to me." He was such a hothead that I often felt uneasy about what he might do. But I also got some insight into the depth of feeling that traditionally binds together a boss and his henchmen in Japanese underworld gangs.

During this time I had a technical commission with the army and navy, one of the privileges of which was to be able to eat at the officers' mess. In the autumn of 1943, when I was dining at the navy base at Yokosuka, I heard the young commissioned officers say that Japan had been defeated at Guadalcanal. "The Americans are advancing on Japan and will overrun it like a tidal wave," one said. "But before that happens I'd like to take a submarine and attack the Panama Canal." So the situation is hopeless, I thought. It was hard to accept. In 1944 I was summoned by the military command of the navy after the sea battles off Taiwan. The staff officers sat in a long row, and I was told to sit down in front of them. The navy's destroyers had been equipped with a new sonar system supplied by NEC, but one after another they were being sunk by enemy submarines. "This sonar is produced in your plant," I was told, "And because of its faulty performance our destroyers are being sunk." It was almost an accusation. If I was going to be punished anyway, I might as well say what I thought, I decided, and boldly argued back: "It's not the sonar we produced that is at fault but the way you are using it. Surely, you need to retrain the sailors." I should add that the enemy had developed a strategy whereby two or three submarines would join forces. One of them, acting as a decoy, would raise its periscope, with the result that the Japanese destroyer, sighting it, would chase after the sub at full speed. At speeds higher than twenty knots the sonar would fail to function because of the noise. The other enemy subs would wait for that moment, then fire a torpedo into the side of the destroyer.

Hearing my counterargument, the staff officers remained silent; then one lowered his voice and said, "You are right, but we have no time to retrain." I realized then that defeat was inevitable. And yet the official announcements remained unchanged: "Japan is winning. We are winning." I left the room very somber.

THE GREAT AIR RAID

At the beginning of 1945 the clouds of defeat began to darken. Before long the enemy would be landing in Japan. And yet I had had no time even to evacuate my family. I decided to pack a few clothes and send my wife and children off to the country. A young engineer at the company agreed to help me. At night during the blackout, as we groped around in the darkness packing the bags, this young engineer suddenly blurted out, "Japan is beaten." Instinctively I looked around me in case the military police might have overheard. In those days everyone was afraid to say what we all wanted to say.

Because NEC itself was busy evacuating its Tokyo plants, the production of weapons dropped sharply. Air raids increased in frequency and widened in scope. I still have clear memories of the great air raid of May 23. A huge formation of more than two hundred U.S. B29s attacked Yokohama. Then a group of them flew over Tokyo. Almost every day I slept at the plant, but that evening I happened to be at home in Himonya. The air raid began about midnight and went on for two hours. I got my family into the temporary air-raid shelter I had built in the garden and, holding my fireman's axe, watched anxiously as the B29s flew overhead.

As the air raid drew to a close, one lone bomber came hurtling past directly over our house. Then there was a whistling sound. My god, it's a bomb! I thought, and braced myself. But I heard no explosion. I turned around and to my astonishment saw a hundred-pound bomb stuck in the ground almost at my feet. Terrified that it was a delayed-action device, I got my family to safety, but it proved to be a dud. Because of that one unexploded bomb, however, my outlook on life changed completely. My life had been saved. If the bomb had exploded, not only I but all my family would have died. This narrow escape made me realize how insignificant my life was. Strangely, all my anxiety disappeared and I felt much calmer. It is no exaggeration to say that I looked at life in a totally different way after this incident.

Although the bomb appeared to be a dud, it might have exploded at any time. Full of concern I reported it to the police at the civil defense headquarters. They were nonchalant. "Do what you think best," they said, adding only that I might evacuate all the neighboring houses within three hundred feet of the bomb. Their irresponsibility struck me as amazing.

My family had moved to Himonya in 1941. Right after I was married we lived at Okuzawa; after that we moved to Jiyugaoka and then to Nishi Ogikubo. We moved to a different section of Tokyo once every two years. The house at Himonya had originally been a dance studio, and as a private residence it was quite large for that time. Misled by its apparent opulence a burglar broke in once. He later confessed to the police, remarking that our house might have been big, but there was precious little to steal in it.

During the war we were often unbearably hungry. Next to the house in Himonya was a grove of oak trees. We once gathered acorns, ground them in a stone mortar, and tried to eat them. But they tasted like sand, so we never tried them again. My weight, which had been over 180 pounds before the war, went down to 110 pounds and I was bordering on malnutrition. I couldn't even climb the stairs at the office without holding on to the handrail.

By July 1945 almost the entire plant at Kawasaki City had been moved to the countryside. My wife and our two preschool daughters had been evacuated to a village near Tokyo. My oldest daughter and son had been evacuated with their schoolmates to a temple in the Ina Valley, in Nagano Prefecture. On July 24, 1945, I received a double appointment as assistant manager of the Otsu Plant in Shiga Prefecture and head of the Underwater Acoustic Products Plant in Kawasaki, and I set off to take up my post in Shiga.

When I left Tokyo I was given special treatment as a civilian in military service and was able to get train tickets easily. Thinking that perhaps I would never see my children again alive, I boarded a train for Ina. I couldn't hold back my tears when I saw how emaciated my two oldest children had become. Although my son survived those difficult times, in 1964, just after he had completed his master's degree at Tokyo University, he fell ill and died. He was only twenty-six, the same age as my younger brother Teiji had been when he died. The faces of my son and my younger brother still live on in my heart like two sides of the same coin.

I arrived in Ina on the day the war ended. With the emperor's announcement that the war was over, the world I knew was totally changed. I was at Ina Station about to board the train for Otsu with my specially procured tickets, but all of my special privileges had suddenly ceased to exist, including my right to railway tickets. Military men, and civilians attached to the military, would be allowed to board only after ordinary passengers. I ran to the station master. Fortunately he understood my situation and squeezed me onto the jam-packed train. I arrived safely at my new post at Otsu, but by then NEC was close to collapse. I took charge of the plant, but with work at a standstill I had nothing to do.

3

LAUNCHING INTO THE WORLD MARKET

UNDER THE OCCUPATION

Two months after the war ended, my duties at the Otsu plant also came to an end. I was appointed assistant manger of the Tamagawa plant and returned to Tokyo in late October 1945 only to find the plant occupied as an important wartime installation. A squad of U.S. soldiers carrying guns loaded with live ammunition was stationed there. Although the Japanese had capitulated completely and had no desire whatsoever to resist, for the American occupation forces this was still a battle zone. We had no idea what would happen, and it was my job to see to it that nothing did.

A steady stream of exhausted Japanese soldiers began to return from the front. Soon there were more than two thousand men at Tamagawa. At the end of December the newly appointed manager of the plant arrived, and the following month the head office began to discuss plans for rebuilding the company. The Tamagawa plant, it was decided, would build all-wave radio receivers as well as the communications equipment that we had been producing up until then. It was the president's order, the manager told me, that we come up with a plan to build twenty thousand all-wave radios a month. We had neither money nor materials—indeed, we had nothing at all. How could we possibly plan for production on such an enormous scale? On the other hand, how could we disregard the president's direct orders? I suggested that we begin with a plan to build five thousand sets a month. The president was furious and the manager, who was in poor health, stepped down. I replaced him.

Even making five thousand sets would be difficult, so we started off with a target of a thousand a month. Later the head office stopped production and disposed of the goods in stock at cut-rate prices. Although I was in charge of production, the head office had made the decision without informing me. I could scarcely contain my outrage at the management for behaving so irresponsibly. NEC had tried making radios for household use in the midtwenties, but had stopped just before I entered the. company. Now they had withdrawn from the field a second time.

About this time NEC's president, Takeshi Kajii, and the managing director, Yasujiro Niwa, were purged by the General Headquarters of the Allied occupation forces. Such purges were one of the consequences of Japan's defeat. Another managing director, Nagao Saeki, became president, but soon he too was purged and executive director Toshihide Watanabe was appointed president in his stead. Though my colleagues and I weren't even directors, we had to assume direct responsibility for managing the company. The year was 1947, and I was just forty years old.

As manager of the Tamagawa plant, the first thing I had to do was to negotiate the removal of the American soldiers stationed there. I approached the headquarters of the occupation forces in Yokohama and begged them to move the squad somewhere else. I was greatly relieved when my request was granted.

Meanwhile at the plant radical labor groups were holding protest rallies from morning till night. According to the demonstrators I was a representative of the capitalist class. Hungry and emaciated, I made a pretty pitiful capitalist. The demonstrators did not confine their activities to the plant; they even came to my home. Once they asked my wife what my monthly salary was. "Forty-five hundred yen," she told them, and soon the union was broadcasting that figure over the plant's loudspeakers.

Actually I received only four thousand yen a month from the company. Even though I held the top-ranking position at the plant, salaries were determined by the number of family dependents one had. I earned four thousand yen and ranked only eighth on the payroll. But since I couldn't support my family on that amount, I had disposed of some of my personal belongings and was thus able to hand over an additional five hundred yen each month to my wife. But she was unaware of that fact.

NEC was in total disarray and had to take action to cut costs right away, so it decided to cut back on personnel. Three hundred workers were to be laid off at the Tamagawa plant alone. I made the rounds of all the factories in Kawasaki City and was able to find jobs for almost all of these workers. The smaller companies had plenty of work; it was the large ones that were in the worst shape.

Dismissing workers was a difficult task in those days; one actually put one's life at risk by doing so. I had heard many stories about managers who had been hauled up before a kangaroo court of workers, or had had their faces burned with lighted cigarettes, or had been beaten until they were bloody. Things did not seem to be as bad as that at my plant, but I certainly felt in danger and was unsure about what would happen next.

I begged the security guards to protect me if the worst came to the worst. The guards agreed, but only if I would promise to vouch for them if they should happen to beat anyone to death in the process. Since I could hardly give them that assurance, I made a noncommittal reply. The police were powerless. Indeed, because authority over them had been transferred from the national to the city level, the police themselves were angry. "I'd rather not work at all than be a lackey for the mayor," they grumbled. I asked them to protect me but to no avail. Though I had served as the president of the local police auxiliary, I now resigned from office. What was the point of having police at all if they were not there when you needed them?

I decided to build a hidden escape route out of my office and installed a trapdoor behind my desk. If trouble occurred during a dispute and any ruffians should force their way in, I would reason with them as best I could, but if persuasion failed I could escape through the trapdoor.

One day a man came into my office wearing the white band around his body that gangsters wore. "You fired me, Kobayashi," he said. "Tell me what clause in the Labor Standards Act gives you the right to do that?" The question of whether to run or stand my ground was purely academic, since he was coming straight at me and I had no time to escape. "Please forgive me," I said and threw my arms around him. This seemed to catch him totally by surprise. For a moment he stared at me nonplussed, then he said, "You can't fool me, Kobayashi," and left the room. I never did get to use my escape hatch.

Because we had absolutely no work at the plant, a strike, which took place in September 1947 for a pay raise, didn't have much meaning. The union members suffered terribly. Some became peddlers; others went around putting on plays or doing any odd jobs they could. After a month they had become totally exhausted and the strike came to an end.

THE CARRIER TRANSMISSION SYSTEM

By the end of 1947 NEC was on the verge of bankruptcy. Rumors were even circulating that the current finance minister had told a cabinet meeting there was no point in trying to save NEC. Our only hope was to ask for help from the Reconstruction Finance Corporation, a government financing agency. Even there, however, the atmosphere was not favorable to NEC. But one young man who had survived the Guadalcanal sea battles urged that the corporation send an investigating committee to check out the Tamagawa plant before making its final decision.

When I heard that a group composed mainly of members of the Reconstruction Finance Corporation was coming to Tamagawa, I made an appeal to the union. "This is our last chance. When the committee makes a tour of the plant, pretend you are working as hard as you can." The union members wanted to keep their salaries, so they pretended to be hard at work. Just before the end of the year the corporation approved reconstruction funds for NEC.

At the occupation forces' General Headquarters (GHQ) was a man called W. S. Magil, whom I had heard of before the war when he was a quality-control engineer at Western Electric. One day Magil called me into GHQ and immediately began to speak. "Because Japan's communications facilities are in such poor shape, we can't maintain public law and order. The main reason for this is that the vacuum tubes used in long-distance telephone circuits are defective. NEC, which supplies those vacuum tubes, should completely upgrade its vacuum-tube production methods by introducing a quality-control system. If you are interested, I will show you how to do it myself."

I had heard about statistical quality control when I first entered NEC so I knew something about it, but I had not been very impressed. Now, however, I immediately accepted his offer. And that is how quality control began at NEC. I suspect we were the first company in all of Japan to introduce such a system. It is well known that after the American statistician Dr. W. Edwards Deming visited Japan in 1950, the Japan Union of Scientists and Engineers promoted the use of quality control. In November 1952 NEC was awarded the Deming Application Prize.

Around 1948, when war broke out in Vietnam between the Vietnamese army and the French forces stationed there, the French army placed a large order with us for portable radio-telephone sets. For a factory with no work to do, that order was a godsend. Because inspection of the devices was to be conducted in French, I was greatly indebted to President Watanabe, who could speak the language.

The plant was still in a state of great confusion because of transfers of men and matériel made during the war, and our technical team had not yet returned to full strength. Yet during this time the company's central research laboratory kept many able engineers on the payroll with almost no research to do. I suggested to the president that the central research laboratory be temporarily disbanded and its engineers mobilized to reinforce the engineers at NEC's two plants at Mita and Tamagawa. Once we were back on our feet, the central research lab could be set up again. He adopted my proposal and reallocated a number of talented engineers to the Mita and Tamagawa plants. We now had the organization to tackle the work. The central research laboratory started up again in 1953, bigger and better than it had been before.

One day in 1950 I was summoned to GHQ by Colonel E. F. Hammond. Without going into any details he asked me to start work on portable carrier transmission equipment right away. "When do you want it?" I asked. "In a week's time," he replied. "That's impossible," I said. "How long will it take, then?" he shot back. Caught up in his excitement, I promised to deliver it in a month.

Hammond was a military man and used to making quick decisions. When he told me to make the system right away, I realized something serious had happened. But the workers at the plant had not fully recovered from the dislocations caused by Japan's defeat. All was in chaos, and I couldn't be sure that we could make the deadline for what was obviously an emergency situation. As a last resort, I asked him to send me a squad of GIs, and the squad arrived at the Tamagawa plant the next day. The workers seemed startled, but when they learned about the emergency order from the occupation forces, they immediately set to work. When we completed production right on schedule one month later, Colonel Hammond made an inspection tour of the plant. For me that month had been a series of crises. Only later did I discover that the communications system we had been ordered to produce was for the Korean War.

Microwave Communications and TV Broadcast Systems

The ability to develop products that will break new ground is the key to the future for any business. Even during the period of confusion following the end of the war, I often discussed this matter with my engineering colleagues. The two areas in particular that I had my eye on were microwave communications systems and television broadcasting systems.

Already during the war Japan had developed an ultrashort-wave radio system and made it available for practical use. Kenjiro Takayanagi and other engineers at NHK (Nihon Hoso Kyokai, the Japan Broadcasting Corporation) had been actively working on television. Under instructions from the Ministry of Communications, NEC had even been engaged in making a trial model of a coaxial cable transmission system for broadcasting television programs from Tokyo to Osaka. History has no room for the word *if*, but if war had not broken out with China in the thirties, television broadcasts would have been relayed from

Tokyo to Nagoya and Osaka by the late thirties or early forties.

In 1947 we decided to meet the challenge of developing a microwave communications system. Because NEC had a business relationship with the International Telephone and Telegraph Corporation (ITT) in the U.S., we were able to produce domestically the pulse time modulation (PTM) system that ITT had developed. Once the system was completed, we had to find a customer somewhere to use it. I concentrated on the electric power companies because NEC had a past record of successes in supplying power-line carrier telephone systems to them.

I finally asked for an interview with President Ungoro Uchigasaki of the Tohoku Electric Power Company. Although I had previously approached many of his subordinates about using our system, it was clear that they were waiting for him to give his approval. President Uchigasaki told me, "I don't understand this microwave system of yours, but I am overwhelmed by your enthusiasm. It will be awkward, though, if it doesn't work, so please build it at NEC's expense." A contract was duly drawn up with the proviso that Tohoku Electric would purchase the system if it worked satisfactorily.

I returned to Tokyo immediately and reported to President Watanabe. "I take full responsibility," I said. "Please let's have a go at it." The microwave circuit between Sendai and Aizu Wakamatsu was completed in a year. One noteworthy incident occurred during the construction. Sukehiro Ito, who was an NEC microwave engineer, got lost in a blizzard at Mount Hayama. The local police sent out a huge search party to look for him. Fortunately Ito had taken refuge in a farmhouse and was able to wait for the snow to stop.

Of course Tohoku Electric lived up to its agreement and purchased the system. Ours was the first microwave circuit in operation in Japan. Prior to this, as I recall, Japan National Railways had installed a microwave circuit across the Tsugaru Straits between the islands of Honshu and Hokkaido, but because of technical difficulties they were slow in putting it into use.

I remember another incident involving microwave circuits. The Nippon Telegraph and Telephone Public Corporation (NTT—now privatized and renamed the Nippon Telegraph and Telephone Corporation) was thinking of using a microwave system developed by the British company Standard Telephones and Cables. The president of NTT at the time was former NEC president Takeshi Kajii. We asked him to give domestic makers a chance. He compromised by first having a domestically produced system installed between Tokyo and Osaka and then putting in an imported system between Osaka and Fukuoka. The Tokyo–Osaka circuit using NEC products was in operation two years ahead of the Osaka–Fukuoka link, to the great credit of supporters of domestic production.

The new technologies of the postwar era were microwaves and television. Although in Germany the use of microwaves was forbidden by the Allied occupation forces, there were few such restrictions in Japan, and those were in force only during the early postwar years. Television was prohibited, however. Makers in related areas of Japanese industry initiated a campaign to persuade the Allied forces to permit television broadcasting. In his newspaper President Matsutaro Shoriki of the Yomiuri Shimbun Company stressed the importance of commercial television broadcasting in addition to the government-supported network NHK. President Shoriki proposed a "mountaintop method" that would use microwaves to relay a broadcast from mountaintop to mountaintop. We at NEC, however, favored a method of overcoming interference from mountains by taking advantage of radio-wave diffraction.

In 1953 NHK began regular television broadcasts, using American-made broadcasting equipment supplied by RCA. The first stirrings of commercial television broadcasting in Japan also began about this time. Believing that commercial broadcasting facilities should be made with Japanese technology, I made direct appeals to all the parties involved. At first I tried to sell our equipment to the Osaka TV Broadcasting Company, but I could not convince its president, Tsuyoshi Suzuki, to break his rule against being the first to use a new system.

Forced to look elsewhere, I turned my attention to Chubu Nippon Broadcasting Company and visited President Kureo Sasabe in Nagoya. President Sasabe was a man of vision. All he said when he promised to use our system was, "You're absolutely sure it will be all right, Kobayashi, aren't you?" To celebrate I invited President Sasabe to the famous Nagoya restaurant, Kawabun. The hostess whispered to me that Mr. Sasabe likes to recite *gidayu*, a traditional form of ballad-drama, so I asked him if he wouldn't sing for me. After that, Mr. Sasabe, in high spirits, told me to "keep up the good work." And that is how we supplied the very first domestically produced television broadcasting equipment to the Chubu Nippon Broadcasting Company.

I had complete confidence in our broadcasting equipment, but we had little experience with television antenna engineering. I went to Tokuya Fujita, assistant director of the NHK Science and Technical Research Laboratories, and promised to pay whatever it cost if they would give us their help and guidance. I got a favorable response.

We also eventually supplied television broadcasting equipment to Osaka Television Broadcasting. Broadcasting equipment thus came to occupy one sector of NEC's business activities. Demand for microwave systems expanded from use in communications to use in television relays. Our prospects now looked bright for emerging from the chaos of the immediate postwar period. By 1952 NEC regularly began hiring university graduates.

WORLD STRATEGY

I spent the 1952 New Year's holiday working on my message for the coming year. I wanted to call on the employees to make NEC's Tamagawa plant the best in the world, but upon further reflection that seemed a bit unrealistic. In those days it would have been hard to claim that we were the world's best, so I changed the phrase to "best in the Far East." Yet I could not suppress the feeling that my aim was indeed to become the best in the world. In my New Year's address two years later I did in fact urge my employees to make NEC the best company in the world. A company the size of NEC could no longer survive on just the Japanese domestic market alone. Somehow or other we had to go out and challenge the world. I added the phrase to my speech because I wanted our employees to think on a global scale.

In 1954 President Watanabe decided to go on an inspection

tour of several foreign countries. His secretary and two NEC directors, Takeshi Ozaki, the manager of the Mita plant, and I from Tamagawa, were to accompany him. Perhaps he thought that by taking Ozaki and me we could cover all the important areas. For the president of a Japanese company to go on an extended business trip to Europe and the U.S. with two of his directors was very unusual in those days. When the trip was announced in the newspapers, NEC's stock prices plummeted.

Our itinerary included the United States, Great Britain, France, Germany, and Italy. We traveled around the world in search of leads for the future development of NEC, browsing through novelty shops in downtown New York and buying unusual items to bring back to Japan with us in much the same way that tourists in Tokyo today wander around the electronics stores of Akihabara. How times have changed!

The prime purpose of our trip, however, was to tour companies affiliated with International Telephone and Telegraph, which was a major NEC stockholder, and to hold friendly discussions with chief executives in the ITT group. ITT was then one of the world's leading manufacturers of communications equipment. NEC was number one in Japan. If NEC were to launch itself into the world market, the two companies would become competitors. Because ITT had absorbed the overseas operations of Western Electric in 1925, NEC's cooperation with ITT was based on the understanding that the two American companies enjoyed a close relationship. But was that understanding correct? For a long time I kept thinking we needed to look into the situation more closely.

It was important not to jump to hasty conclusions, yet what precisely was the relationship between Western and ITT? This question nagged at me constantly as I met with officials from both companies. After a while I learned an important fact. During World War II ITT's status had changed and it had begun competing with Western in the world marketplace. I therefore advised President Watanabe to think of them as two completely independent companies. NEC had concluded a licensing agreement with Western through ITT, but now that the relationship between the two had changed, it seemed advisable to enter into a contract directly with Western.

When NEC had been founded as a joint stock company on July 17, 1899, Western held 54 percent of the stock equity, and the remaining 46 percent was held by Japanese investors including Kunihiko Iwadare and Takeshiro Maeda. Thus, despite outward appearances NEC was in fact an operating division of a foreign company. In 1932 it became a Japanese company both in substance and in name. But until the early 1960s ITT was NEC's single largest stockholder. After that it divested itself of all its NEC stock.

I have many memories associated with Western Electric. In 1958 when I was a senior vice president of NEC, I visited J. V. Dunn, who was in charge of patent licensing at the Western head office. Although I told him I wanted to meet his superiors, he refused to introduce me. "My superiors are extremely important people," he said. "They don't have time to meet someone like you." I visited Dunn's office every day and one day a tall man came in. Dunn stood stiffly at attention and said, "Yes, sir." After the man had left, I asked Dunn who he was. It turned out to be Joseph R. Bransford, the executive vice president of Western.

Some short time later I introduced myself to Bransford and requested an interview. "I was in Mr. Dunn's office when you came in the other day. My name is Kobayashi and I am an executive at NEC, a Japanese company created by Western at the end of the last century." Bransford invited me into his office. Later Dunn quit Western. We invited him to work for NEC and he consented. Relationships between people sometimes evolve in mysterious ways.

Bransford introduced me to the president of Western. After I met the president, I was able to meet all the other company officials informally in the executive dining room. Sometime later I decided I would also like to meet the executives at AT&T, Western's parent company. I had heard that Haakon I. Romnes, chairman of the board at AT&T was the same age as I was. But although I had the people at Western ask to arrange a meeting to discuss "advances in Japanese telecommunications," no such arrangements were ever made.

I met Chairman Romnes quite by accident one day when I was invited to a luncheon meeting with executives from the

43

Chemical Bank. Who should be sitting next to me but H. I. Romnes. I turned to him and said, "I am the same age as you. I've wanted very much to meet you, but so far without success." Romnes's reply was simple: "Anytime." Once I had met Romnes, it was an easy matter to meet the other executives at AT&T. By meeting as many people as possible and building a network of relationships, I was able to raise public awareness of NEC. That is my way of doing things.

In April 1954 the twenty-fifth reunion of the graduates of the Tokyo University Electrical Engineering Department was held at Alumni Hall in Tokyo. The album of family photographs, which had become an established custom at our tenth and twentieth reunions, was again very popular.

Overseas Markets

Any major undertaking takes at least ten years from the time it is conceived to the time it can stand on its own. If NEC was going to enter the overseas marketplace, we could not afford to sit around and wait. We had to begin immediately. NEC already had advanced microwave communications technology; perhaps this would be useful to the developing countries.

As a first step I visited Taiwan in 1956. At that time speaking Japanese was still to be avoided in Taiwan, yet we needed to build a foothold for our operations there. After discussing the matter with President Watanabe, we decided to enter into a joint venture with local Taiwanese capital. Our partner was to be Chen Maopang, but he was a commercial capitalist and thus not an ideal partner for a manufacturing company like NEC. After some discussion we switched to Lin Tingsheng, with whom we had more in common. After this change the venture proceeded smoothly.

Having concluded that a joint venture with Korean capital would also be best for our dealings in Korea, we formed two joint companies, one with Samsung to produce electron tubes, the other with the Gold Star group to make telecommunications equipment. I became very close friends after that with Byung-Chull Lee, chairman of Samsung. He died in 1987, and in

December of that year I made a visit to his grave in Yong-in Farmland to pay my last respects.

In the mid-1950s, I also traveled around Southeast Asia, visiting Thailand, Vietnam, Cambodia, and Laos. These visits did not lead immediately to business talks, however. Three of these countries were former French colonies that had only recently gained their independence. I remember the Cambodian minister of postal services complaining that after he had dismissed all the French engineers, the country was experiencing difficulties with its telecommunications services.

In 1956 or thereabouts I received a letter from Professor Shintaro Uda of Tohoku University asking NEC to donate a two-thousand-megahertz microwave system to the National Physical Laboratory in India where he had been invited as a guest professor. I consulted President Watanabe, and NEC donated the equipment. As a result of Professor Uda's request, NEC entered into contact with Bharat Electronic and Indian Telephone Industries. In 1959 we received a huge order for a coaxial cable carrier system from the Indian Ministry of Communications.

Our undertakings in India thus expanded from microwave communications systems to coaxial-cable carrier systems, but it was a broadcasting system of ours that brought our relationship even closer. One day the Indian authorities approached me with a special request. "We want the manufacturing know-how for a medium-wave broadcasting system. But we not only want to produce this equipment in India, we want to export it as well. That will mean we will be competing with NEC. We would like to enter a technical agreement with you based on that understanding."

This request required thinking over, but I advised President Watanabe to provide the technology India asked for. NEC had succeeded by importing technology from abroad. If the developing countries should grow and become our competitors, we should welcome the competition but try to keep one step ahead of them. Since that time we have always maintained friendly relations with India and have worked to expand our business there.

After India came Pakistan. In 1962 we received an order from Pakistan for a coaxial-cable carrier system. From there our market expanded to Iraq.

To go back a bit in time, we had supplied a microwave communications system to Indonesia in 1959. Because that vast island nation had practically no telecommunications facilities, rice might cost twice as much in one place as it did in another. I advised the Indonesian authorities to upgrade their telecommunications system and suggested that the microwave equipment produced by NEC was the most suitable for their purposes. From those beginnings the project to link all the islands of Indonesia by microwave was born, and NEC was in a position to move ahead with it.

We had a very close call on one of our Indonesian projects. The first Asian Games (now known as the Asian Olympic Games) were scheduled to open in Jakarta on August 15, 1962. President Sukarno planned for the games to be televised, and placed an order with NEC for a broadcasting station and all the necessary equipment. Although we were given an unusually short period in which to complete the project, by working around the clock we were able to finish everything at noon on August 14, the day before the games were to begin. But no sooner had we finished than our sighs of relief turned to gasps of horror as the Indonesian-designed steel tower on which we had mounted a broadcasting antenna weighing several tons began to sway dangerously. By the time we had finished the repairs it was late at night. We met our deadline for the games with only a few hours to spare.

A year earlier, in 1961, NEC received the contract for a large telecommunications project in the Philippines under Japan's war reparations program. Originally it was scheduled to be a two-year "turn-key" project involving the installation of automatic switching systems at central telephone offices in and around Manila. Although we pushed ahead diligently with our end of the work, unexpected problems arose on the Philippine side that greatly delayed the completion of the project. We learned a useful lesson, however, in the importance of project management. Our subsequent record in project management improved greatly, and we even attracted world attention in that area. It was a case of "practice makes perfect."

Feeling that now was the time to think about markets on a global scale, I turned my attention to Central and South America. Our first job in that part of the world was an order from the

46

Mexican Ministry of Postal Services to deliver and install a microwave communications system. I knew Mexico only from what I had read in books but had no firsthand knowledge whatsoever of the land itself. The microwave communications system was to be installed not only in the cities; it would also have to pass through steep mountains and isolated valleys. I decided to walk along the installation route, and so with a feeling of adventure I set out for Mexico in 1963.

Much to my surprise all the relay sites along the route were accessible by jeep. In Japan I had done a considerable amount of walking when we installed microwave systems. In some places there weren't even any footpaths, let alone roads. In my experience Japan seemed to have more jungles than Mexico.

Not all my ventures abroad went smoothly, of course. I was once involved in a swindle and was sued by an international con man in Guatemala. The trick had been a simple one. Between the end of the document our representative had signed and the place for the signatures was an area of blank space that the con man had later filled in as he pleased. I finally summoned him to Mexico City and met him with Taizo Kawakita, who was my assistant in charge of NEC's overseas business. "Be careful," Kawakita warned me. "He may have a gun in his briefcase." After that alarming suggestion I went into the meeting in fear and trembling.

After a few failures such as this one, I gradually became more astute in my dealings abroad.

COMPUTERS

In 1954 one of our young engineers, Hitoshi Watanabe, developed a new design theory for wave filters, which were an important component in the multiplex carrier telephone systems NEC had been producing since before the war. After announcing his theory at a learned society, Watanabe made a direct appeal to me: "In order to apply my theory to an actual wave filter, I need a calculator capable of handling figures of twenty-two or twenty-three digits." Watanabe's theory was a series of formulae that I could not decipher, but I decided we had to have a computer for this sort of project. Sooner or later, I believed, NEC would be entering the computer field.

The type of computer Watanabe wanted was not yet available in Japan. Just about that time, though, Eiichi Gotoh, an assistant (later a professor) in the School of Science at the University of Tokyo, invented the parametron, a type of resonance circuit that was cheap and dependable. Kyozo Nagamori and his colleagues in NEC's Electronic Machine Laboratory pressed ahead with the development of computers using the parametron and finally succeeded in building a parametron computer capable of doing scientific calculations, including the sophisticated numerical computations required by Watanabe's plans for a wave filter. Meanwhile, we developed a small parametron computer for business use called the NEAC-1201. It was highly acclaimed; its only flaw was its slow operating speed.

I knew that Hiroshi Wada of the Ministry of International Trade and Industry's (MITI) Electrotechnical Laboratory, was developing a computer that used transistors. I visited Wada and asked for his help. Wada gladly complied. That was how the NEAC-2201 came into being. When it was completed in 1958 we decided to display the new computer in Paris the following year at the Automath exhibition during the International Information Processing Conference. Since there wasn't much time, we shipped the computer by plane to Paris entirely at NEC's expense. It was the first functioning transistor computer ever to be put on public display. Even now I think back on it with pride.

In 1960 Nagamori and I went abroad to visit computer makers in the U.S. and Europe. Our ultimate aim was to ascertain which of the leading companies would be best for NEC to enter an affiliation with. When we went to Machines Bull in France I encountered the word *software* for the first time. One of the executives at Bull gave me a word of advice: "Software is indispensable for running computers," he said. "But creating it takes a lot of time and money. Japanese makers are convinced they can make a profit without worrying about software, but that's crazy. If they let themselves be dazzled only by the hardware end of the business, they're sure to fail." I knew what he was saying, but it was much later before I really understood its full implications.

When I returned to Japan I reported to President Watanabe

*My father, Tsuneo, elementary school
principal and later village headman.*

My mother, Den.

Graduation from Matsumoto High School, March 1926. I am seventh from the right, standing at the back. The wooden school building is the clubhouse.

With professors and classmates in a laboratory at the Tokyo Imperial University, 1927. I am sixth from the left.

Just married: Koji and Kazuko Kobayashi (middle front), on March 10, 1935.

Aboard the Queen Mary en route to New York, March 1938; my first business trip abroad. I am fifth from the left.

Paris, 1954, with Mr. Takeshi Ozaki, a plant manager (center), and Mr. Toshihide Watanabe, president of NEC (right).

With my family, 1954: from the left, Kimiko, Teiko, Makoto, Noriko, and Kazuko.

As president of NEC, announcing my management plans to NEC executives, November 30, 1964.

The dedication of the NEC microwave communications system acquired by U.S. forces to cover the Kanto Plains in Japan, 1969.

At Electropia 70, held at NEC's Yokohama plant, 1969, in commemoration of the company's 70th anniversary.

With my wife, at the Empire State Building,
New York, January 22, 1965.

that the Minneapolis-Honeywell Regulator Company (now Honeywell) in the U.S. was the most suitable partner for us. After further study we entered into negotiations with Honeywell, and in 1962 we received governmental approval for a technical tie-up with the company. As a result NEC had not only its own computers, developed in-house, but also a line of computers based on licensed technology, with the result that we were able to supply a full range of machines from small to large. We received nearly one hundred orders for our medium-sized NEAC-2200 computer that appeared in 1964, making it our best-seller. This was renamed model 200 of the NEAC-2200 series when this series of family machines was announced in 1965.

Following the favorable start of its computer operations, NEC soon led the field among the domestic Japanese computer manufacturers and was trying to catch up with powerful foreign-capital manufacturers, such as IBM, in terms of Japanese market share.

In May 1965 NEC announced the NEAC-Series 2200 computer family in competition with the IBM System 360, which had made its debut in April 1964. The NEAC-Series 2200 was available in five models. All these models were tailored after the "one machine" concept, ranging from a small model 100 to a large model 500, and sharing the same hardware and software architecture.

The NEAC-Series 2200 model line was later extended. Capitalizing on the trend toward more computers in various societal activities, NEC was able to consolidate its position and occupy the mainstream of the computer business from the 1960s on.

The course of history takes some strange and unexpected turns. In March 1987 NEC, Honeywell, and Groupe Bull jointly founded Honeywell Bull in the U.S. The three companies are working together to offer a computer to the American market that will be independent of IBM.

SEMICONDUCTORS

NEC's semiconductor business traces its origins back to our work with transistors. Our research laboratories, which had reopened in 1953, developed alloy-based transistors and point-contact transistors made from germanium. We began production the following year.

Other manufacturers in the field were planning to mass-produce transistors using licensed American technology. Opinions at NEC were divided and the company was vacillating about the course we should take. Some felt we should develop transistors based on our own original technology, and our research people seemed quite confident of success. Although I couldn't fully agree with them, it was a new technology and I didn't have the confidence to voice a strong opinion of my own.

The person in charge at MITI was pressing me for our decision. "Other companies are importing U.S. technology," he said. "What does NEC intend to do?" After consulting with President Watanabe, we decided to import the technology from GE. We immediately submitted an application to MITI, and without waiting for the authorization to come through, I set off for the U.S. with Teruo Hayashi, a semiconductor engineer. We were in New York when official approval for our application was granted. That was in December 1958.

Quite independently of these negotiations, I had had a special factory built in one corner of the Tamagawa plant, to be used exclusively for the production of transistors. This special facility, the first of its kind in Japan, went into operation in April 1958. Though from today's perspective it is only a small factory, an investment in plant and equipment of that magnitude was a big risk for NEC at the time.

Although germanium was the primary material used for transistors in those days, NEC was the first in Japan to switch to silicon, which today has become indispensable in the production of semiconductors. Two reasons led us to focus on silicon. NEC intended to use transistors in communications equipment rather than for home appliances. Silicon could be used at higher temperatures and was more reliable than germanium. That was our first reason. Transistors were evolving into integrated circuits (IC), which are made by mounting a number of transistors on a wafer. Creating these circuits requires delicate manufacturing techniques, for which silicon is better suited than germanium. That was our second reason.

Although there are also difficulties involved in working with silicon, by good fortune we were able to solve them all. In 1960 NEC succeeded in developing the world's first silicon transistor for use in telecommunications. The patents for the silicon planar process, which plays an important role in the integration process, were held by Fairchild Camera and Instrument Corporation in the U.S. NEC acquired exclusive licensing rights for their patents in Japan in 1963. Those patents gave us tremendous power and laid the foundations for our rapid advance into a position of leadership among the world's makers of semiconductors.

THE BEGINNINGS OF SATELLITE COMMUNICATIONS

When I was in the U.S. in 1958 I learned that ITT had succeeded in building a communications link without the use of relays across 140 miles of sea between Florida and Cuba. The method used was troposcatter waves. Disturbances in atmospheric density in the troposphere cause radio waves to scatter. The use of these waves makes it possible to build an over-the-horizon radio communications system for long-distance transmissions. The U.S. government would not allow the ITT system to be used within the continental United States, however, because the transmitter had an output of ten kilowatts, which would cause interference with other radio transmissions.

If we could develop a high-sensitivity receiver, we could reduce transmitter output and use the troposcatter for communications within Japan. When I returned to Japan, I discussed the matter with some NEC engineers. Masasuke Morita and Sukehiro Ito had the answer. If we used the high-sensitivity receiving system that Morita and Ito and their colleagues had developed, we would need only one hundredth of the output required by the ITT system. Using the Morita-Ito system we completed an over-the-horizon communications system for all of Japan, including the southernmost islands of Okinawa. Improved high-sensitivity receiving equipment would later form the basic technology for satellite communications.

The first people to react to our system were a group of researchers at an IBM laboratory working on data transmissions via radio in the suburbs of San Francisco. We agreed to let them use our new equipment for their experiments. This was the beginning of high-speed computer data transmissions by means of our over-the-horizon system.

Our high-sensitivity system was responsible for yet another NEC success story. In the mid-1960s the U.S. Far Eastern Air Force was planning to build a communications network in the Kanto area around Tokyo. Bidding was limited to U.S. firms, but NEC asked to be allowed to participate. "You can submit a bid," we were told. "But your estimates can be only half as much as the American companies'." Despite these harsh and indeed humiliating conditions, NEC won the bid. The reason for our success was quite simple: Only NEC had the technical capability to meet the air force's requirements. The U.S. companies concerned had to use the high-sensitivity receiving system NEC had developed. I urged everyone to stick to the deadline in order to win the air force's confidence. As a result, we delivered the system two months ahead of schedule.

I was summoned to Washington by the U.S. Air Force to receive a huge incentive award for beating the deadline—the first time in air force history, I understand, that such an award had been given. U.S. newspapers carried articles about it. The next day I received a telephone call from a U.S. university asking for a donation. A day later another university called with the same request. NEC donated half of the two-hundred-thousand-dollar award to two American universities and allocated the remaining half to support NEC employees who wanted to study overseas. That made everyone on all sides happy.

In the summer of 1962 I received a major shock. I was in a hotel room in Chicago, and when I turned on the television set views of Paris appeared on the screen. The artificial satellite *Telstar* launched by AT&T was being used to relay scenes from Paris live to the U.S. The event was being hailed as the most brilliant achievement since Charles Lindbergh's solo flight across the Atlantic.

On my way back to Japan I stopped in at the Hughes Aircraft Company in Los Angeles and told Lawrence A. Hyland, vice president of Hughes, of my deep disappointment: "Something I have dreamed about for a long time has already been accomplished. I've lost my chance." Hyland then showed me a mock-up of a geostationary satellite made by one of his engineers, Harold A. Rosen. "If we launch three of these satellites," he said, "we can communicate with any place in the world." Because *Telstar* was a low-orbit satellite, its relay range was limited. When I looked at Rosen's plans, the scales dropped from my eyes. I immediately accepted Hyland's proposal that Hughes and NEC work together to develop satellite-communications technology using geostationary satellites.

In Japan KDD, the country's international telecommunications company, was already proceeding with tests of a transpacific communications system using *Relay*, a medium-altitude satellite developed by RCA. NEC was cooperating with KDD on this venture. In November 1963 KDD succeeded in receiving its first TV transmission from America. What should appear on our television screens but the tragic news of President Kennedy's assassination. Our elation at this technological triumph turned instantly to shock and dismay.

The greatest event for Japan since the end of the war was the Tokyo Olympics of October 1964. Why couldn't we use geostationary satellites to broadcast the Olympics live throughout the world? I wondered, and approached the authorities with my idea. Their reaction was far from encouraging. "It's impossible," I was told. "We are too pressed for time." I then went to NEC's President Watanabe and asked him to get permission to let NEC do it on its own.

The Japanese government allowed NEC to install transmitters and antennas at the Kashima Satellite Communication Earth Station, part of the Ministry of Posts and Telecommunications's Radio Research Laboratories; NEC assumed the entire expense of the project. On the American side Hughes Aircraft rebuilt the Point Mugu Naval Air Station north of Los Angeles and used it as a receiving center. That was how Japan and the U.S. were able to see the first live satellite transmissions of the Olympic Games. These broadcasts were taped in Los Angeles and sent from there to Canada. Transmissions to Europe were sent by ground circuit from Los Angeles to Montreal, where they were taped, then sent by air to Hamburg and broadcast in twenty-one European countries.

One of the achievements of which I am most proud is providing the satellite-communications technology that contributed so much to the success of the Tokyo Olympics.

4

TACKLING INTERNAL REFORM

BECOMING PRESIDENT OF NEC

When the Olympic project had been completed I at last had a chance to relax a bit. It was the autumn of 1964 and I was just a few months short of my fifty-eighth birthday.

One day President Watanabe summoned me into his office. As I stood in front of his desk wondering what new job he had in mind for me now, he suddenly stretched out his hand. Without understanding what he intended, I extended my own hand. He grasped it and said, "Kobayashi, you're our next president."

The news was so sudden that I didn't know what to say. The stockholders' meeting was only two days away. As time passed, I began to feel increasingly overwhelmed by the enormity of what had happened. November 30, 1964, is a day I will remember for the rest of my life. The stockholders' meeting began at nine o'clock and was followed by a meeting of the board of directors, where I was officially appointed president of NEC. My first order of business was to attend a press conference at the Industrial Club of Japan in the Marunouchi section of Tokyo. "I want to make NEC into an international corporation," I said. It was my first official pronouncement as president.

The next day I began a tour of the company's major plants to address the employees. I asked Mr. Watanabe, who was now chairman of the board, to come with me. "I may say a few things you won't like hearing," I told him. "But please just listen and don't say anything." He willingly agreed. The two of us went around together to the NEC plants in Mita, Tamagawa, Sagamihara, and Fuchu. In his speech as outgoing president Mr. Watanabe recalled the confusion of the postwar period and reminisced about the eighteen years he had served as president since taking over from Nagao Saeki in 1947. "We have finally reached the stage when we have bright prospects for future development. Ever since I reached sixty-five, I have thought of withdrawing one day from the front ranks. That day has finally arrived."

When my turn came I praised Mr. Watanabe for his hard work and for the distinguished service he had rendered the company, then I launched into my first speech as president. This, I realized, was a crucial moment. If I let this opportunity escape, any hope of management reform would be lost. I had to make a clean break here and now.

For some time I had felt something verging on a crisis mentality at NEC. Although we were maintaining respectable business results, we were also facing mountains of problems. We had exceptionally capable personnel, but we were not using them to their full potential. Something had to be done right away. If we waited any longer, it would be too late.

But where to begin? NEC had twenty-three thousand employees and sales of 70 billion yen. A company this size could not be run by a single individual. It was far beyond one person's powers. My top priority, I decided, was to rectify this organizational flaw.

"From point to area"—that slogan summed up the first target of my management reforms. Every company executive with the rank of senior vice president or higher would serve as the president's alter ego, sharing all information with him and enjoying his complete trust. As president I would occupy the central point of the management circle. The senior executives would be situated around the circumference; from there they could manage their divisions more effectively, I believed, than a centralized president could. It was this circular concept that found expression in the phrase "from point to area."

The concept came to occupy a central position in my ideas

on management. Playing with a pun on the word *top*, I later renamed it my "top theory." Because each division of a company acts independently and develops in its own way, it exerts a centrifugal force. But, just like in a spinning top, there must be a countervailing centripetal force to maintain equilibrium and preserve the integrity of the company as a whole.

The executives in charge of each decentralized division, who compose the surface area of the top, are responsible for striking a balance between these centripetal and centrifugal forces and, in their capacity as the president's alter ego, for dealing with most management problems. The president and chairman of the board are located at the center like the spindle of a top and form the main axis of the company's management functions. That in essence is my "top theory" of management.

I started out by trying to convert the company's executives to my way of thinking at our twice-weekly corporate management committee meetings. But they didn't seem to understand what in the world their new president was talking about. I had a hard time getting my ideas across to them, but I had made it a rule that all internal reforms would start at the top and move downward. This was to avoid any unnecessary confusion and to prevent unrest among the employees. I also announced that for the time being I would make no personnel changes.

The year closed in a flurry of activity. Just before the end of 1964 I received a long-distance call from the U.S. It was my good friend Dr. Jack A. Morton, vice president of Bell Laboratories and the inventor of the Morton tube. The eleventh National Symposium on Reliability and Quality was being held in Miami. "Would you be willing to address the symposium," Dr. Morton asked me, "and discuss the secrets behind the high quality of Japanese products?" Shortly after his telephone call, I received an invitation to President Lyndon Johnson's inauguration in Washington. This was an opportunity not to be missed. In January 1965 I flew to the U.S.

President Johnson began his inaugural address by saying, "Ours is a time of change . . . Even now, a rocket [the *Mariner 4*] moves toward Mars." I shared his perceptions of the times. When I returned home I urged my employees to be "more dynamic and more flexible."

MANAGEMENT REFORM

The second target of management reform was to perfect our system of operating divisions. Although a division system had been introduced into the company in 1961, only half-hearted efforts had been made to create a unified cooperative relationship between the plants that were responsible for engineering and production, and the marketing division, which was in contact with the customers for our products. The division of responsibility between our line operations and our central staff was also unclear. It was a division system in name only.

The new system that I was proposing was a more streamlined arrangement. The general manager of each division would be the company president of the division in his charge. Each division would act as its own profit center and be fully responsible for its own profits. By such an arrangement I thought I could change the traditional management pyramid into a horizontal, disk-like structure.

The problem with a pyramid-shaped hierarchy is that it takes too much time and effort for any information to reach the president's ear. Not only does information have to trickle up the ranks through general managers, section managers, and senior staff, it usually must pass through acting managers and deputy chiefs as well. With a clearly defined authority figure on top, the lower echelons are all too often cowed into submission, and no one is willing to take the initiative. I had worked my way up from the lowest levels of such a hierarchy and knew only too well what it was like down there.

I therefore divided the entire company into approximately fifteen divisions. Each of them would be consolidated around the axis of its own particular market and field of technology and limited in scope to make it easier for its general manager to run.

I was in a hurry to establish an adequate division system as soon as possible. In May 1965 I made an official announcement about personnel and administrative reforms. I called together everyone concerned and explained my policies to them over and over again. I personally wrote up memos on the subject, which I passed around to NEC executives in an attempt to make them understand. I must have written some twenty memos on management-related matters alone.

The front ranks eagerly awaited the president's new policy. In Japan employees are highly dedicated to improving the company they work for. In order to live up to my employees' expectations I proposed a ZD program for the entire company. *ZD* stands for "zero defects," a program proposed for America's defense industries by Robert McNamara, who was then U.S. secretary of defense. I had learned of it when I was touring a company in the U.S. Each workplace within NEC formed into teams that set goals for themselves and began working to eliminate any defects.

That summer I was in Karuizawa attending a seminar for top-level executives. In the middle of the conference I received a telephone call from my wife in Tokyo that a major magazine was carrying an article on my zero-defects program with the big headline: "NEC's Kobayashi Raises Z-flag." The Z-flag is a banner of encouragement, to build up spirit before a naval encounter. In the spring of 1966 Kakuzo Morikawa, president of the Japan Management Association, came to ask for my help in organizing a national zero defects campaign. I readily consented and have supported the movement ever since.

"Nippon Electric does it the U.S. way" was the title of an article in the December 11, 1965, issue of *Business Week* on NEC's new management policies—perhaps because they seemed to reflect an American-style efficiency. When I think about the U.S. fascination with Japanese management principles some ten years later, I can't help but suppress a wry smile. Despite the article's title I doubt whether there is any manager as thoroughly Japanese as I am.

In April 1966 the chairman of the board, Toshihide Watanabe, died at the age of sixty-nine. He had not only been an authority on labor issues but was a man of wide-ranging interests who spoke French very well and had served as the chairman of the Japan High School Song Festival Committee.

That same month I addressed the joint national convention of Japan's four major electrical engineering institutes on the topic

"Japanese knowledge industry from the standpoint of the electronics industry." The Japanese economy was then in a period of high-level growth centered on heavy industry, but I predicted that knowledge and information would be the economic mainstays of the future. My starting point was the theory of Professor Fritz Machlup of Princeton University, which had been first propounded in his 1962 book *The Production and Distribution of Knowledge in the United States* and later popularized by Gilbert Burck in an article in *Fortune* magazine.

Professor Machlup's thesis was that the key to industry and society from now on would be education, plus research and development—in other words, knowledge. Many years later the information economist Marc Porat would corroborate this thesis by tracing changes in U.S. employment patterns to show the advance of information-related activities. Other thinkers who discussed the idea of an information society include Alvin Toffler and John Naisbitt. I firmly believed that knowledge also held the key to NEC's future corporate identity, though it was sometime later that I developed the concept of "C&C"—the integration of computers and communications.

Back in 1961, whenever I entered the executive dining room, my colleagues, who had up until then been enjoying animated conversations, would suddenly fall silent. This happened frequently enough to bother me, so I set out to discover what they had been talking about. The answer was golf. At that time golf was just beginning to be popular in Japan, but I had had no time to learn how to play. Apparently out of concern for my feelings my colleagues tried to change the subject whenever I appeared, but that proved difficult to do and an uneasy silence would fall instead. Not wanting to cause them any embarrassment I decided to try golf myself. I found it a lot of fun to play and, besides, it was good for my health. So at the age of fifty-four I took up the game.

In 1969 NEC celebrated its seventieth anniversary. As part of the celebrations the executives held a golf tournament. I had a net score of seventy-seven (I had been given a handicap because of my age), and thus the president of the company was declared the winner—although with all those sevens the win was a bit too good to be true.

NATIONWIDE DECENTRALIZATION

The system of divisions envisioned in the "from point to area" movement was an attempt to develop NEC's management structure in a horizontal rather than a vertical direction. If management was to develop horizontally, then our plants ought to spread out too—there was no need to concentrate them all in the Tokyo-Yokohama area. I decided that after 1965 our new facilities would be built in all parts of the country. I called this our nationwide decentralization plan. Under it NEC would have three types of plants: Type A, with fifteen hundred employees, to be built near large cities; Type B, with a thousand employees, to be located in medium-sized cities; and Type C, with five hundred employees, for smaller cities.

If we were going to decentralize at all, we might as well begin by moving to relatively remote locations—Ichinoseki, in Iwate Prefecture, to the north, and Izumi, in Kagoshima Prefecture, and Kumamoto City, Kumamoto Prefecture, to the south. If we could succeed in those three places, which were more than six hours away from Tokyo by train, surely we could succeed anywhere else. NEC Kagoshima and NEC Kyushu were established in September 1969; NEC Tohoku in Ichinoseki opened the following June.

Despite the distance between these regional plants and the Tokyo head office, we should have no problems if we used the communications systems that NEC itself made. As the saying goes, we couldn't let the shoemaker's wife go barefoot. As a maker of communications equipment it was important to set an example by using our own technology. These new plants and the jobs they provided would also do their part in preventing depopulation in the countryside and overcrowding in the big cities.

As a general principle each regional plant was to be an independent corporation. Not only would it be more efficient to allow each plant to operate autonomously; given their remote locations it would be impossible for representatives from the head office to make frequent visits anyway. Decentralization would also be useful in fostering a sense of independent initiative. While

I was president of NEC we built eleven regional subsidiaries; since I became chairman of the board we have built an additional fifteen.

When did the society and economy of postwar Japan reach the turning point? Even today that is a hard question to answer. But for me the turning point came in 1969. In September of that year the International Industrial Conference was held in San Francisco. While I was there I met Dr. Aurelio Peccei of the Club of Rome, the advocate of "limits to growth." I will never forget the discussion I had with him in the lobby of the Fairmont Hotel, where the conference was being held. "You must have children and grandchildren, Mr. Kobayashi," he said to me. "But if the world continues the way it is today, the human race will be in a pitiful state in the twenty-first century as far as food supply and pollution are concerned. It is not too late. We still have time to do something. Won't you join us?" Saburo Okita, head of the Japan Economic Research Center (now chancellor of the International University of Japan), also urged me to join, and so I became a member of the Club of Rome.

I felt most sympathetic to the spirit of the Club of Rome not only because of its eager interest in the future of humankind, but because of my admiration for the behavior of European intellectuals. As I understand it, they often exchange ideas on particular issues as occasions demand, irrespective of national borders, and put them into action when an agreement is reached. I thought it imperative that the Japanese learn this manner of absorbing and exchanging ideas and taking necessary actions. We should understand what the word "club" means in this context.

A few years thereafter the Club of Rome, Japan Committee, was organized in Tokyo and the late Mr. Kogoro Uemura, Chairman of the Japan Federation of Economic Organizations, was made president. Since then, breakfast meetings have been held from time to time to talk about matters of common interest. I have been president of the Club of Rome, Japan Committee, since April 1987, when Mr. Uemura passed away.

The theme of the 1969 International Industrial Conference was the role of the chief executive officer. The discussions proved very informative. It is my firm belief that the CEO's role is to help the corporation to grow, to give it an image that will be favorably received by society at large, and to see to it that it can perpetuate itself.

Another fruit of the conference was my warm friendship with Fletcher L. Byrom, president of Koppers Company. His nine commandments of management I found extremely edifying:

1. Hang loose.
2. Listen for the winds of change.
3. Increase the number of interfaces.
4. Keep your intuition well lubricated, but
5. Make sure you know where the information is buried.
6. Use growth as a means of getting and keeping good people, and use those people as a means of achieving continued growth. The two are interdependent.
7. Avoid like the plague those specialists who are *only* specialists.
8. Set your priorities in terms of the probable, rather than the merely possible, but
9. Make sure you generate a reasonable number of mistakes (because rectifying them will keep you on your toes).

The mid-1960s and early 1970s were a time of violent change for Japan. The period of high-level economic growth reached its climax with Osaka EXPO '70 in 1970, but several ominous signs had already begun to appear that suggested this growth could not be maintained. I felt the time had come to tighten the reins on NEC's corporate expansion.

As if to confirm my forebodings, in August 1971 President Nixon announced that the U.S. was going off the gold standard—one of the events of that summer usually referred to in Japan as the "Nixon shocks." The yen was set free to find its market level, and by December of that year the exchange rate, which for nearly twenty years had been 360 yen to a dollar, was suddenly down to 308 yen. NEC had no choice but to cut its exchange losses by disgorging the earnings it had been so carefully accumulating.

The prophets of gloom in the mass media were predicting zero or even minus growth for Japan. But I believed that even though it would be impossible to maintain the high-level growth we had hitherto known, we could at least hope for an appropriate growth rate that would be sustainable with a minimum of ups and downs. Accordingly, both within the company and outside it I began to use the expression "stable growth."

OPERATION QUALITY

About this time I was made chairman of the management planning council of the Japan Committee for Economic Development and set about drawing up a model corporate identity capable of coping with the new social climate. The council deliberated for two years before submitting a proposal in March 1973 entitled "Toward the Establishment of Mutual Understanding Between Business and Society." In the process of composing this proposal I carefully considered the problem of corporate accountability to society from my vantage point as a corporate manager and gave serious thought to how we at NEC should develop. In any case we had to do something to counter the growing tendency to brand big business as the villain.

By the end of 1971 I had worked out NEC's own management guidelines, using improvement of the quality of life as our basic criterion. In January 1972 I announced to all our employees that Operation Quality would go into effect immediately. From then on we at NEC would pursue not only quantifiable goals but demand quality as well. In those days merely proposing such a program in the broadest of terms, even within the company, took considerable courage.

In my New Year's address of January 4, 1972, I called on the employees to enhance the quality of all NEC's undertakings by pursuing the following seven goals:
1. Quality of management capability and performance
2. Quality of products and services
3. Quality of work environment
4. Quality of community relations
5. Quality of employee attitudes and behavior
6. Quality of business achievement
7. Quality of corporate image

I also set forth my ideas on Operation Quality in that year's business report to our Japanese stockholders and in our annual report in English. I remember how gratified I was to receive letters from top executives of important U.S. firms who said they shared my views entirely. In November 1974 I was awarded the Deming Individual Prize for Operation Quality, which was cited as a unique development of the quality-control movement. Even as recently as October 1985 I was invited to the Quality Day Symposium held by Bell Laboratories to discuss Operation Quality and the results it had achieved.

CULTIVATING OVERSEAS MARKETS

In fiscal 1966 NEC's overseas sales topped the 10 billion yen mark for the first time. That year our foreign sales amounted to 10.7 billion yen and accounted for 10.6 percent of the amount sold by the entire company. In those days Japan regarded the increase of exports as an important contribution to the national economy. Every year NEC was officially commended by the Ministry of International Trade and Industry for its services in this area, and in 1964 I personally received the meritorious services award for export promotion from the prime minister.

As I mentioned earlier, NEC's overseas operations had begun in southeast Asia and from there had expanded both geographically and in terms of the types of equipment we sold. Because the benefits of telecommunications are not confined within the borders of a single country but can cross national boundaries and provide links to the rest of the world, I firmly believed that communications systems would continue to grow and develop until a global information network had been completed. Possession of advanced means of communications, moreover, would also lead to improvements in a country's industrial output, economy, and standard of living.

Although NEC sought opportunities to make itself useful in this area, we had to face the harsh reality that American and European manufacturers were better known and had more actual overseas experience than we did. It was going to be a difficult job to make our presence felt in the international marketplace. We would have to fight hard to win a competitive edge through nonprice factors such as quality, after-sales service, and a rigid adherence to deadlines.

Believing that it was more effective if the president himself went out to meet prospective customers, I decided to visit as many places as possible. In 1964, the year I took office, I made two overseas trips for a total of twenty-three days. The next year I went abroad three times and was away for forty-eight days. In 1966 I made six trips, and in 1967 eight, for a total of sixty-three and ninety-five days respectively. Although not all of these trips were for business purposes, their steadily rising number is one indicator of NEC's tilt abroad.

This was the era of the DC-8 plane, but in time it became possible to fly from Haneda Airport in Tokyo nonstop to the West Coast of the United States, without refueling in Hawaii, and then directly to New York City. I never found foreign business trips a hardship, however, perhaps because I am not particular about what I eat. When in Rome, do as the Romans, they say, and because food is the ultimate expression of a country's or a region's culture, I strove to build friendly relations over the dinner table.

As our exports increased I began to realize the need for local production overseas. Not only would this deepen our understanding of local conditions within the countries we were doing business with, but the countries themselves were starting to express a strong desire for domestic production. My rule of thumb was to "branch out to wherever we are welcomed." Thus we set up corporations to produce communications equipment in Mexico and Brazil in 1968 and in Australia the following year.

I made my first visit to Australia in 1963 to bid for the 930-mile microwave system that country was then planning to build between Brisbane, the capital of Queensland, and Cairns, in the northern part of the state. Francis P. O'Grady, director-general of the Australian Post Office, whom I met on that occasion, was a truly dedicated man. Because of the importance of the project, not only did he listen attentively to what I had to say, he even made a personal visit to the NEC plant to check out the equipment for himself. Only after he had seen with his own eyes the powerful new microwave system NEC was offering did he tell me he was satisfied and place the order with us. I was deeply impressed by his sincerity and strong sense of responsibility. In April 1966 a splendid ceremony was held in Brisbane to mark the completion of the microwave network. This marked the beginning of other large-scale orders for NEC microwave systems.

One day Mr. O'Grady said to me, "If you really want to understand the importance of communications in Australia, why don't you begin by going to Alice Springs? It's a small town in the middle of the vast deserts of central Australia, but there is still a relay station there from the Overland Telegraph Line, the country's first north-south communications link. I strongly urge you to go because I don't believe you will ever be able to understand the distinctive character of Australian communications without first seeing Alice Springs."

Since Mr. O'Grady was so insistent, I decided I had to go to Alice Springs, so I boarded a series of small planes and visited the site of the telegraph station. Though located on quite a daunting communications route, it undoubtedly proved serviceable to many, many people. In Australia, I understand, telegraph stations like this one are dotted throughout the country.

While I was there I went to see Ayers Rock. This giant monolith, far removed from the rest of the world, is 1.5 miles long, a mile wide, and over one thousand feet high. It is said to change color seven times a day as the sun moves through the sky. I was overwhelmed by its magnificence, which was far beyond anything in my experience in Japan. But that was all a long time ago. Today NEC has three subsidiaries in Australia with more than two thousand local employees.

In nearby New Zealand, I have vivid memories of the July 1971 opening ceremonies for a satellite-communications earth station NEC had built in pastureland about forty miles north of Auckland. As the ceremonies were drawing to a close Mr. Allan McCready, the postmaster-general of the New Zealand Post Office, rose to his feet and unexpectedly announced, "President Kobayashi, because you have contributed greatly to New Zealand's development through the construction of this satellite-communications earth station, we would like you to be initiated into the Maoris." I knew that the Maoris were the native people of New Zealand who even today take great pride in their traditional way of life, but I felt slightly apprehensive about what was going to happen next.

The postmaster-general led me to the door of a room and said, "Kobayashi, the Maori rites are very solemn and sacred. Only the initiated can go beyond this door. I'm sorry, but you'll have to go in alone. Good luck." It was too late to turn back now, so summoning up my courage I stepped into the room. About a dozen or so powerful-looking Maoris, splendidly dressed in native attire, were sitting there holding sharp spears in their hands and staring intently at my face.

Steeling myself I stood in front of them. As I did so a man more distinguished than the rest moved forward, said something in the Maori language, then had me swear something in English. Then all the Maoris stood up and, shaking their spears at me, began to speak in Maori. Although the occasion was one of celebration it was difficult not to feel alarm, but fortunately the rite ended without bloodshed and I became an honorary Maori. After the initiation was over and I returned to my seat, I received the congratulations of all present. I remember bowing my head in thanks to Mr. McCready, who had brought the ceremonies to such a splendid conclusion by arranging this hair-raising event.

As I mentioned earlier, in 1968 NEC established a wholly owned subsidiary in Brazil. The following year I flew there via New York to attend the September 4 opening of a plant for making crossbar switching equipment in a São Paolo suburb. I still remember thinking how beautiful the red NEC logo looked against the chalk-white wall of the newly completed building. Responding to the words of greeting from the local authorities, I expressed my thanks for the warm welcome they had given us and emphasized the importance NEC placed on contributing to the upgrading of Brazil's communications infrastructure. I did feel a bit self-conscious, however, because the new plant was only eighteen thousand square feet and had only 150 employees—a very small plant indeed. But to me it was the embodiment of my philosophy of "Start small and grow big."

As our business abroad expanded, the number of our overseas construction sites increased markedly. Because communications has the potential to link together all the countries of the world, improve the quality of life, and extend the scope of human knowledge, I felt it my personal mission to be of some service toward the ultimate fulfillment of these goals. But I worried about our engineers in the field, where a sense of mission alone could hardly compensate for the extreme conditions under which they had to work. One of our engineers operating in a mountainous area of Iran once told me, "I sleep in my van at night and set off for work in it the next day." When I started to apologize, he replied, "But it's all in a day's work." There was nothing I could say to that.

One day an NEC engineer was conducting the final tests on a one-hundred-kilowatt medium-wave transmitter that we had built in the middle of the Iranian desert. Just then the shah of Iran, Mohammed Reza Shah Pahlavi, arrived to make an on-site inspection. The tests proceeded without a hitch, and the engineer returned home to Japan. Sometime later the shah, through the intermediary of the Iranian ambassador in Tokyo, conferred the Order of Iran on this NEC engineer.

In November 1967 we succeeded in winning a contract from Iran to build a seven-route microwave communications system. This mammoth project involved constructing a microwave network twenty-five hundred miles long and the stations for it, as well as training the necessary personnel to operate it. At the Iranian government's request, we were to set up a joint venture, and I was to be granted an audience with the shah. The Japanese ambassador to Iran accompanied me and gave me a few words of warning. "Kobayashi, this is the *shahan* shah you are meeting today, so don't start chattering away like you usually do. Just bow and keep quiet, and after a minute or two we'll leave."

When we arrived in the presence of the shah, he looked at me and said, "Do sit down." I glanced over at the ambassador. It was a clear case of "damned if I do and damned if I don't." The audience lasted a half hour, and I vividly remember the passion and enthusiasm with which the shah discussed the "White Revolution," his plans to industrialize Iran. The joint corporation was established in 1971 and built a carrier transmission equipment plant at Shiraz in the southwest part of the country.

The order we received from Iran in 1970 for an integrated national telecommunications system, called INTS, was another large-scale project which involved the construction of a microwave network eighty-seven hundred miles long. Because the successful completion of the project was thought to be beyond the powers of NEC alone at that time, an international consortium was formed consisting of NEC, two companies from the U.S., and one from West Germany. This was a cooperative venture well befitting the dawn of the age of internationalism.

I consider the period from 1970 to the present as the era of global expansion for NEC's business operations. Inevitably this has meant certain qualitative changes in the way we do business. I have already written extensively about our overseas ventures involving communications equipment and other communications-related projects. From around 1970, however, we no longer confined ourselves to communications but broadened out to include electron devices, especially semiconductor devices; home electronics; and computers. Achieving a good balance both in the types of equipment a company offers and in the geographic distribution of its operations, I believe, is the secret of risk-avoidance in the business world. This was perhaps our foremost change.

The second qualitative change arose from the sudden emergence of an overseas consumer market for our products. To strengthen our marketing system we first set up an Overseas Terminal Equipment Marketing Promotion Division in August 1978, followed by similar organizational shakeups. As a result of these efforts the overseas sales of our mass consumer products, which since 1975 had been struggling for supremacy with our systems products, gained ascendancy in 1980 and have maintained it ever since.

The third qualitative change has been the expansion of our operations on a worldwide scale. In order to further reinforce our long-standing encouragement of local production, I believe the time has come for NEC not only to offer goods and services on the markets of the countries where our overseas bases are located, but to upgrade our overseas operations by establishing a division of labor among our production bases everywhere, including Japan. In the section entitled "An International Corporation" I will introduce specific examples of some of the methods we have adopted.

Launching the
Satellite-Communications Business

The new frontier of communications is satellite communications. My presidency at NEC coincided with the company's formal entry into the satellite-communications field.

On December 6, 1965, we conducted ground simulation experiments of the STAR system (an acronym for *satellite telecommunication with automatic routing*) at the Tamagawa plant. Joseph V. Charyk, president of the Communications Satellite Corporation (Comsat), and Allen E. Puckett, vice president of Hughes Aircraft, came to Japan to attend the demonstration. STAR was a multiple-access system that enabled several earth stations to relay communications to a single satellite equipped with a transponder capable of transmitting automatically upon reception of a signal. NEC had the technology in all the required areas—radio, ground stations, and switching—and put this expertise to use to develop the new system.

On May 30, 1966, in cooperation with Hughes Aircraft, we opened an experimental satellite-communications earth station for the STAR system in Hot Springs, Arkansas. Masahisa Miyagi was instrumental in building this station. Just at that time the International Telecommunications Satellite Organization (Intelsat) was holding a conference in Washington, D.C. We invited eighty representatives from the thirty-two participating countries to Hot Springs for a public demonstration. This series of events impressed the world leaders in this field with our technological expertise and zealous commitment to satellite communications, and contributed greatly to the orders for earth stations that NEC received later.

Comsat, which had been founded under the terms of the U.S. Communications Satellite Act of August 1962, was the manager of the International Telecommunications Satellite Consortium. Through the intermediary of Japan's international telecommunications company KDD, Comsat asked me to send a Japanese engineer to work with them. I selected Tadahiro Sekimoto, then head of our Communications Basic Research Laboratory and now the president of NEC. For two years, from August 1965 to September 1967, Sekimoto served in Comsat's laboratory and participated in the development of the SPADE system (an acronym for *single channel per carrier PCM multiple-access demand-assignment equipment*), the world's first digital satellite-communications system.

Our first order from abroad for a satellite-communications earth station came in 1967 from the government of Mexico. It was used to televise the Mexico Olympics in October 1968. NEC was responsible for supplying transmitting and receiving equipment and for integrating the system as a whole. The antenna production was allocated separately to the Mitsubishi Electric Corporation. I was soon hearing complaints that Mitsubishi had affixed a large company logo to the antenna so that everyone thought it was responsible for the entire earth station. Thereafter, I made it a point for NEC to provide the entire system, antenna included.

In June 1968 we received an order from Peru and opened a station there despite difficult working conditions and many anxious moments. Although we had learned our lesson in Mexico and had contracted for the whole system, some of our Japanese subcontractors reneged on delivery because our standards for the antenna were too demanding. Hurriedly we hired an American maker. Later we bought the necessary technology from an American company that specialized in antenna panels and set up our own antenna-production system.

The following year, on July 20, 1969, the U.S. *Apollo 11* spacecraft succeeded in landing on the moon. The only country in South America to be able to see live broadcasts of those first historic lunar views was Peru. Despite a sudden change in frequency allocation, NEC had been able to adjust the frequency of the Peru earth station to allow for reception. I believe this was one reason why I received the Grand Cross of the Government of the Republic of Peru in 1969.

After that NEC's reputation continued to grow as we opened earth stations in Australia, Kuwait, and Taiwan in 1969 and in Jordan, Singapore, and New Zealand in 1971. At home in Japan we opened new stations at Kashima and Juo in 1968 for the Ministry of Posts and Telecommunications and KDD respectively, and the Yamaguchi station in 1969 for KDD. In this way, satellite communications established itself as one of NEC's new business areas.

In 1972 diplomatic relations between Japan and China were normalized, and Prime Minister Kakuei Tanaka was to visit Beijing to sign the treaty. In July of that year I proposed to the Ministry of Posts and Telecommunications that we have live satellite coverage of the public ceremonies surrounding the resumption of diplomatic relations between the two countries. NEC was in complete possession of the technology to build a small-scale earth station using an antenna only thirty-three feet in diameter. The ministry was less than enthusiastic, however, because the prime minister's visit was only two months away and because no funds had been allocated for such a project.

I decided that NEC should go ahead with the satellite transmission on its own and consulted with our engineers and specialists in the field. They felt that we could probably manage by diverting some of our already-existing equipment to the project. "The prime minister of Japan is going to China. We must succeed in broadcasting this historic moment at all cost." With these words I rallied our employees behind me and once again raised the Z-flag. Because diplomatic relations between the two countries were involved, this was one job that did not permit a single mistake. We dismantled a transportable earth station that had been assembled at the Yokohama plant and sent it to Beijing on a Japan Air Lines DC-8. The People's Republic of China gave us its complete cooperation. The station was set up alongside Beijing Airport in just three days. Usually assembly takes more than a week.

Finally the big day arrived. On September 25, 1972, Prime Minister Kakuei Tanaka walked down the ramp of a special Japan Air Lines jet at Beijing Airport and Premier Zhou Enlai stepped forward, clapping, to greet him. Then came the signing of the friendship treaty and the banquet at the Great Hall of the People. All of these historic events were relayed frame-by-frame live to Japan and televised throughout the world. The earth station that NEC had hurriedly erected in Beijing had more than adequately served its purpose.

With this success the activities of NEC's satellite-communications operations gathered momentum. The transportable earth station that we had taken to Beijing later became the model for

Intelsat's standard small-scale station. NEC ranked first in the world: in the international telecommunications market our share of earth stations amounted to almost 50 percent and exceeded 60 percent for maritime satellite-communications stations. Satellite-communications earth stations grew to be the acknowledged champion of all NEC business operations.

SHAKE-UP IN THE JAPANESE COMPUTER INDUSTRY

In 1970 the world computer industry entered a period of reorganization. That September GE withdrew from the computer business and turned over its computer-related affairs to Honeywell. In September 1971 RCA also withdrew from the field. NEC was aligned with Honeywell, the Toshiba Corporation with GE, and Hitachi with RCA.

At that time six companies in Japan, including NEC, were making mainframe computers. To prepare for the eventual liberalization of the computer business, MITI was urging Japanese makers to work together. The six companies paired off into three groups. In November 1971 NEC announced its affiliation plans and set about developing a new computer series.

Although NEC had a technology-exchange agreement with Honeywell, I had no intention of following Honeywell's system in every detail—ultimately I wanted us to develop our own line. We moved forward with plans for a system that would resemble neither the Honeywell model nor the GE one that Honeywell had taken over. In May 1974 we announced our new series, a line of computers consisting of eight different models. Our small- and medium-sized models came out first, and the larger models proceeded in due course. By April 1976 we had completed our new series, the fastest of the three Japanese computer groups to do so. The series was called ACOS, an acronym for *advanced computer series*.

One day a single large square of thick colored paper was delivered to my office. On it was a Chinese poem about the development of our new series of computers by my middle school teacher Mr. Hojo. Following the rules of Chinese poetry it was composed of four lines. When the first Chinese characters of each line were read together, they formed *Nippon Denki*, the Japanese name of my company. I was deeply touched by my mentor's thoughtfulness and by the care he had taken in crafting the poem.

During this period I was demanding considerable effort from the NEC staff involved in developing the new computer series. But if I relied on someone else's skill to resolve the issues that confronted us, nothing lay ahead but ruin. Only the determination to go it alone makes it possible to break new ground. But how should we proceed with the computer of the future? Should we go ahead with large-scale computers whose size seemed to know no bounds? Or should we go back to the drawing board and rethink the issue altogether? NEC had gone into the computer business because we had realized that computer technology was indispensable for the future development of communications. The electronic switching system of the future would be computers pure and simple.

I had changed the company's organizational structure from a rigid, vertical pyramid to a wide management circle radiating outward horizontally. I had then gone on to expand the circumference of this circle by decentralizing our physical plants and building new facilities throughout the country. Why shouldn't our work with computers take this same horizontal course? At the end of 1976 I came to a conclusion. My idea was a decentralized data-processing system created by linking together a number of small- and medium-sized computers, an approach I called "distributed information-processing network architecture." When I first thought up this phrase I was so delighted I felt I had at last seen the light.

The name was a bit long, though, so I racked my brains for an appropriate acronym. Then one day it came to me in a flash. If I eliminated the p of "processing," it became DINA, just like Dick Mine's popular song "Dinah." "Oh, Dina," I began to sing to myself and expressed all my hopes in that one fervent phrase.

So obsessed was I, I even heard rumors that "the computer will be the death of President Kobayashi." The years following the shakeup of the computer industry until the announcement of DINA were indeed a series of trials for me. But our decision not to pursue compatibility with IBM had proved to be the right course. Today our computer operations are one of the mainstays of NEC.

5

THE SPIRIT OF SELF-HELP

Becoming Chairman of the Board

On April 30, 1976, I left home with a lighter step than usual. I had decided to hand over the NEC presidency to a younger man. At the regularly scheduled meeting of the board of directors, I glanced around at the company officials and began to speak. "I would like to resign as president and become chairman of the board. I propose that Senior Executive Vice President Tadao Tanaka become our new president."

After the OPEC oil shock of 1973 the company had entered a period of stable growth. Tanaka had the strengths in accounting and finance we needed to cope with the new age. He therefore seemed the appropriate choice to succeed me. Another potential presidential candidate had been Takeo Kurokawa, who, like Tanaka, had entered the company in 1937. In 1974, however, when he was executive vice president, Kurokawa had just finished giving a lecture at a company course and was about to go off for a cup of tea, when he collapsed and died instantly of a myocardial infarction.

After the death of the chairman of the board, Toshihide Watanabe, in 1966, I had single-handedly taken charge of both NEC's long-term management strategy and its day-to-day business operations. In American business terms, I was serving concurrently as chief executive officer (CEO) and chief operating officer (COO). But how much longer could I stand the strain? That is why I decided to appoint a COO who would conduct the business along the lines I had already laid down. I was lightening my own workload, which had exceeded my limits, but would continue to hold ultimate responsibility for management as CEO.

The goals I had set had for the most part been achieved. I had done my best to bring three of our business areas—communications, computers, and semiconductors—into the top ranks of world industry. As we entered the second half of the 1970s, our future prospects in those three areas were very bright. Now was the time to make a change. On June 30, 1976, I became chairman of the board.

During the twelve years I was president of NEC, semiconductor devices had developed from transistors to integrated circuits (IC), and from ICs to LSIs (large-scale integration). Since I became board chairman they have developed even further—from LSIs to VLSIs (very large scale integration). Perhaps this is a good opportunity to look back over the history of our IC operations.

In 1966 I decided to make our IC business the nucleus of development of the entire company. I established the IC Design Division that year and concentrated the brains of the entire company in it, gathering together not only semiconductor specialists but also engineers with expertise or experience in telecommunications and computers. To head the new division I appointed Atsuyoshi Ouchi, who in 1988 succeeded me as chairman of the board.

The Nixon shocks of 1971 tested the endurance of NEC's semiconductor operations. Production was down more than 10 percent over the preceding year. Our semiconductor business was able to survive only by having work diverted from other plants. But what ultimately saved it was the use of LSIs for electronic calculators, which were just then beginning to show signs of rapid growth. The decision to produce LSIs for electronic calculators proved a success. In the latter half of 1972 our semiconductor operations were back on their feet again.

The recovery was only temporary, however, because in 1973 came the first of the OPEC oil shocks. Demand for semiconductors plummeted. Rival companies that had been planning to expand their semiconductor plants now appeared to be backtracking. Looking at technological trends, I decided that the market would recover more rapidly than expected. "Now is our chance. Let's do the opposite of everyone else and make heavy investments of personnel and capital in plant and equipment and in R&D." My reading of the situation was correct. Before the first oil shock NEC had ranked second or third in Japan in terms of production volume. In 1974, however, NEC's production of semiconductors was first in Japan with an output of 60 billion yen.

But in order to maintain our lead we needed capital. Semiconductors have an insatiable appetite for money. The tempo of technological advance in that area is dizzyingly fast, and production facilities must be constantly updated. A company that gets behind in research and development will find it almost impossible to catch up. We would not be able to raise enough money from within Japan alone. What were we to do?

Motoo Hirota, who was then senior vice president, and Kenzo Nakamura, associate senior vice president (now vice chairman of the board), proposed that we try to raise funds on the European bond market. At information sessions held in the major cities of Europe, Vice President (now Executive Vice President) Hisao Kanai gave persuasive briefings to the institutional investors attending them. As a result our foreign bond issues sold well, and we were able to finance the expansion of our semiconductor business. By 1984 output had swelled to 590 billion yen, making NEC the largest maker of semiconductor devices in the world.

Around the beginning of 1980 I began to be concerned about President Tanaka's health. He had suffered from high blood pressure, and though he was healthy when he took office, the presidency is an arduous position. Three years later he was showing noticeable signs of strain. Worried that dealing with the aftermath of the second oil shock in 1979 might prove too heavy a burden for him, I appointed Tadahiro Sekimoto to succeed Tanaka as president in June 1980. Sekimoto was fifty-three years old at the time. I had taken the plunge and opted for younger leadership. Tanaka became a corporate counselor.

In the autumn of 1983 Tanaka and I were having lunch together with some other executives in the executive dining room, when he suddenly collapsed. In alarm I tried to help him up, but it was too late.

78

THE PERSONAL COMPUTER BUSINESS

On December 6, 1980, I was sitting in front of a personal computer, tapping away uncertainly at the keyboard. I was quite nervous, not only because this was the first time I had ever used a computer but because there was a newspaper photographer to record my every move. This marked the start of our company-wide Personal Computer Study Group attended by all NEC executives and division heads.

I have always held that the first step toward the integration of computers and communications is to understand the computer and master it for one's own purposes. So one day I said to Atsuyoshi Ouchi, one of the creators of NEC's personal computers, (and now chairman of the board), "Now that we have this convenient device, shouldn't it be more widely used throughout the company? We can't have the shoemaker's wife go barefoot, you know. Let's have everyone learn how to use the computer, beginning with the top executives."

The personal computer I started to learn on was the PC-8001, the first of its kind to be domestically made in Japan. It had been announced to the media on May 9, 1979. Its predecessor was the microcomputer. To understand the history of the microcomputer we must go back to November 1971, when the U.S. semiconductor maker Intel Corporation succeeded in developing a four-bit model, the i4004. NEC's µPD700 series, Japan's first domestically made microcomputer, was completed in April 1972. This was four-bit microcomputer using P-channel elements. Although a system using N-channel elements could do operations more rapidly, N-channel elements were so difficult to produce that hardly any companies had started work on them. The engineering staff at NEC rose to the challenge and succeeded in making the world's first N-channel four-bit microcomputer in September 1973. The following year it announced an eight-bit microcomputer compatible with the one produced by Intel.

NEC began outside sales in 1973 when very few people knew what a microcomputer was. Our sales staff were having a very difficult time. Realizing that something had to be done to improve this situation, we created the Microcomputer Sales Department within the Semiconductor and IC Sales Division in February 1976. Even so we were lucky to sell three hundred computers a month.

The first step was to make the microcomputer better known. As a teaching aid we began selling an assemble-it-yourself eight-bit microcomputer kit, the TK-80 (TK for *training kit*). The kit went on the market in August 1976 for what was then the astoundingly inexpensive price of 88,500 yen. Many in the company expressed doubts about whether a major corporation like NEC should be dabbling in do-it-yourself computer kits. To make matters worse, the kit was packaged in a gaudy cardboard box like some cheap plastic toy. For anyone used to NEC's usual products there was something slightly embarrassing about it.

The first step in our campaign to popularize the microcomputer was to set up a showroom in Akihabara, Tokyo's famous home electronics shopping district. Nicknamed "Bit-Inn" it opened in September 1976—the month after the TK-80 kits had gone on sale. As soon as the showroom opened, any misgivings within the company were dispelled once and for all. So many young computer buffs, even elementary and middle school children, flocked to Bit-Inn that we had trouble supplying enough staff members to answer their questions.

By 1977 microcomputers were becoming established as an NEC business field. Realizing that this greater-than-expected popularization meant we needed a second-source contract with another company, we entered into an agreement with Intel. But as NEC's competitiveness increased and we began to compete with each other in the marketplace, the alliance became difficult to sustain. I therefore handed down the decision that at an early stage we would switch to a proprietary line, and I directed Tomihiro Matsumura (now executive vice president), who was responsible for microcomputer development, to move ahead with the project. That was how work began on NEC's original microcomputer line, the V (for *victory*) series.

To get back to the PC-8001: While NEC was perfecting its microcomputer marketing strategies, three companies in the U.S.—Apple, Tandy, and Commodore—began to sell their own versions of a personal computer. I had to make a decision: Should we enter the personal computer business or be satisfied with the microcomputer kit? I gave the go-ahead to enter the PC business. By the time production of the PC-8001 ceased in January 1983, we had sold a total of 250,000 sets, an unbreakable sales record for a single model in the Japanese personal computer industry. With the PC-8001 NEC acquired the top market share for domestic personal computers, a position we have continued to hold to the present day.

C&C: The Integration of Computers and Communications

In May 1976 I received a shock. Northern Telecom announced the development of a digital switching system at a seminar they were holding at Disney World in Florida. At a gathering of representatives of the telecommunications business from all over the world, Northern boasted it was the only company to be able to provide digital switching.

I had known the president of Northern, Robert C. Scrivener, for many years. He had come to visit me in Tokyo and had proposed that we share our technology and work together to build a digital communications system. I politely refused President Scrivener's proposal. I felt that the time was fast approaching for me to present in a clear and compelling fashion my ideas about the integration of computers and communications. After that visit, however, I should have guessed what was happening, and I can't deny feeling that they had gotten the jump on us.

At the time of the Northern Telecom announcement, NEC was selling crossbar switching equipment and space-division electronic switching equipment on the American market. After the announcement, however, whenever our U.S. sales personnel visited a client they were invariably asked whether NEC had a digital system. As our salespeople began to realize the increasing difficulty of doing business in the U.S. without one, they started to suggest that we put a digital switching system on the market soon. Although I was aware of these suggestions, in view of the fact that Nippon Telegraph and Telephone was committed to a space-division system for Japan, I felt the time was not ripe to make the move to digital switching and decided for the time being to stick with what we had for our overseas markets as well.

Back in 1962 we had built a crossbar switching plant in Sagamihara City, west of Tokyo, that was then one of the foremost facilities of its kind in the world, second only to Western Electric's Hawthorne works. Given the supply capacity of this new plant, we realized that for future business growth we would need to seek markets abroad. The plan to rely on exports to expand our switching equipment business proved a great success on the U.S. market, at least as far as our crossbar switching equipment was concerned. But later our space-division electronic switching system encountered strong competition from Western's No.1 ESS in the U.S., and from ITT's Metaconta 10C system and L. M. Ericsson's AXE in other overseas markets. Fortunately or unfortunately space-division electronic switching proved unexpectedly short-lived, and we entered the age of digital switching.

At the beginning of 1977 the conglomerate TRW took over Vidar, a maker of digital transmission equipment. When Vidar began to sell off its new line of digital switching equipment at rock-bottom prices, executives at NEC America threw up their hands in despair. Although they managed to muddle along somehow, by the summer of that year they knew the situation was hopeless. Unless NEC had a digital switching system, none of their clients would be willing to do business with them. This time, when the request came in from NEC America that we start developing digital switching equipment right away, we had no choice but to join the fray.

In February 1977, while all this was going on, I received a letter from Horizon House, the publisher of a communications trade magazine with head offices in Dedham, Massachusetts, just south of Boston. They were sponsoring the International Telecommunications Exposition (Intelcom 77) to be held that October in Atlanta, and they wanted me to be one of the keynote speakers. Other proposed keynoters included Bjorn Lundvall, president of L. M. Ericsson, the prominent Swedish telecommunications maker, and Robert Scrivener of Northern Telecom.

The main theme of Intelcom 77 was telecommunications and economic development. This was an area of particularly great interest to NEC, and since the exposition was to be held in October I had plenty of time to prepare. Furthermore, in April

I was scheduled to receive the 1976 Frederik Philips Award from the Institute of Electrical and Electronics Engineers for my contributions to the advance and development of electronics and telecommunications. Intelcom 77 would be the perfect opportunity for NEC to make some kind of new departure. Musing over these ideas, I sent off a letter to Horizon House accepting its invitation and set about examining how we should proceed. By now spring was just around the corner.

Fortunately our somewhat hurried development of a digital switching system was proceeding smoothly. Digital transmissions had been in practical use for some time, if we could digitalize all aspects of telecommunications technology, we could improve their compatibility with computers, which were themselves essentially a digital technology.

With the development of distributed information-processing network architecture (DINA) at the end of the 1976 we had been able to create a computer system that could disperse data-procesing functions and data bases to multiple terminals linked together over a digital communications circuit. To press ahead even more vigorously along these lines, we needed to merge the computer with communications. Wasn't this precisely the new departure I was looking for? I would call for the integration of computers and communications at Intelcom 77. Such a proposal would have the added advantage of stimulating our computer business, which had not been having an easy time recently.

I arrived in the U.S. on October 8, flying from London to New York. Fighting jet lag in my hotel room I wrote and rewrote the text of my speech, searching for exactly the right words. I proceeded to Atlanta the following day, and on October 10 I entered the Georgia World Congress Center, where the conference was being held. The title of my thirty-minute keynote speech was "Shaping a Communications Industry to Meet the Ever-Changing Needs of Society." The text I delivered began as follows: "Today, in most developed countries, the telephone and broadcasting services are so much a part of daily life that these nations are already in the information-oriented era. Communiction technology and computer technology are beginning to merge, and the new terminology of computer communication is becoming popular."

Attending Intelcom 77 were the secretary-general of the International Telecommunications Union and the presidents of AT&T, Northern Telecom, L. M. Ericsson, and other major telecommunications companies, yet I was the only one to propose the integration of computers and communications. One hundred years earlier, in 1877, Alexander Graham Bell had invented the telephone. It seemed particularly auspicious to announce the concept of C&C, which I had long been nursing, in that centennial year.

The world was slow to respond to my idea, however. At the time, computers and communications were thought of as two distinctly different types of business, so perhaps the lack of response was only natural. But my self-confidence remained unshaken as I pressed ahead with systematizing the concept and building up the organization for it within NEC.

I am often asked when the concept of C&C first occurred to me. The technological origins of the idea can be traced back to March 1959 and an article of mine entitled "Digital Technology and the Advance of Automation," which was published in a special extra edition of *OHM* magazine. There I argued that the introduction of digital technology would hasten the appearance of large-scale digital systems comprising data-processing equipment and electronic switching, and that when that happened we could look forward to a bright and promising future. Once I had gone that far, all that was left was to try to put C&C into practice within NEC's business operations.

On the afternoon of December 29, 1977, two months after the Atlanta conference, I summoned all our executives involved in C&C-related areas, and a dozen or so division heads, to NEC's conference room and broached the subject this way: "I don't completely understand the interface between computers and communications, but the seeds of technology are in there somewhere. If we don't make a start now, we will be left behind."

This was the beginning of our C&C orientation meetings. Internal restructuring proceeded rapidly as we set up one C&C-related organization after another: the C&C Committee in 1978, the C&C Systems Research Laboratories in 1980, the C&C Systems Unit in 1982, the NEC America C&C Promotion Division in 1983. While the concept was beginning to jell within the company, I went around expounding my ideas not only within Japan but all over the world. Someone even referred to me as the "founder of the C&C religion." In all I gave nearly fifty lectures on the subject.

In October 1978 I was invited to be a keynote speaker at the Third U.S.-Japan Computer Conference in San Francisco. In those days Japanese computers were thought to be mere imitations of American technology. In my speech, however, I traced the roots of NEC's computers back to 1935 and the research on switching-circuit network theory done in the prewar period by NEC engineers Akira Nakashima and Masao Hanzawa. From this perspective on the history of computers I was able to demonstrate the correctness of my ideas on C&C.

Earlier, in May of that year, in a speech marking the thirtieth anniversary of the Japan Electronics Industry Development Association, I had presented my C&C concept in chart form, showing the merging course of computers, communications, and semiconductors. This chart was so clear and easy to understand that it was even cited in a report submitted in October 1980 to the U.S. House of Representatives by the Ways and Means Committee's Subcommittee on Trade.

Large-scale integration is indispensable to the development of C&C. Indeed, as LSIs become even more functionally advanced, their importance has increased. To capitalize on this trend we needed a new organization. In 1978 I had Atsuyoshi Ouchi investigate the possibility of creating one, and in September 1979 we started the System LSI Development Division. As the name suggests, the division carries our hopes not only for further development in LSIs but for their further systematization as well.

Later, when C&C had become common knowledge, the world's leading businesses began to turn their attention to the C&C market. Then, on January 8, 1982, two symbolic events occurred: The U.S. Department of Justice dropped its case against IBM and reached an out-of-court settlement of its seven-year antitrust suit against AT&T. (After many twists and turns, this consent degree would eventually lead to the breakup of the Bell system in January 1984.)

The worldwide attention these events attracted is clear from the special article published in the January 25, 1982, issue of *Time* magazine. A cartoon captioned "Who's Who in the Electronic

Jungle" accompanying the article depicted AT&T as a lion, IBM as a tiger, and NEC—the only non-U.S. firm to be represented—as a crocodile. Perhaps the idea was to present all the leading players in the information and communications markets as caught up in the great surge toward C&C. It was a humbling and somewhat embarrassing thought.

To popularize the C&C concept and support C&C research activities, NEC established the Foundation for C&C Promotion in March 1985. I was appointed president, and well-known representatives of the business and academic communities were asked to serve on the board, seven as directors and nine as trustees. As the highlight of its activities, once each year the foundation honors those who have made significant achievements in the fields of computers and communications.

The first recipients of the foundation's awards, in the fall of 1985, were Dr. Hideo Yamashita and Dr. Hiroshi Wada, the foster fathers of Japan's computers; Dr. Lawrence A. Hyland and Dr. Harold A. Rosen of Hughes Aircraft, the fathers of the geostationary communications satellite; and Dr. Joseph V. Charyk and Mr. Sidney Metzger of Comsat for their contributions to international satellite communications.

The second award ceremony was held on November 7, 1986. One of the three recipients that year was my old and highly esteemed friend, Dr. Jerome B. Wiesner, president emeritus of the Massachusetts Institute of Technology. The two others to be honored were Dr. Izuo Hayashi of the Optoelectronics Joint Research Laboratory and Dr. Morton B. Panish of AT&T Bell Laboratories.

The award citation reads: "As the fields of computers and communications, with their shared basis in the semiconductor, rapidly draw closer together, the integration of their two technologies is hastening the development of the electronics industry. We at the Foundation for C&C Promotion hope that through our activities we may contribute to the future development of the world economy and to the improvement of life in society." As I stood on the podium and spoke these words, my thoughts turned to my friendship with Jerome Wiesner, whom ill health had unfortunately prevented from attending that day.

The foundation presented its third awards on November 26,

1987. The recipients were Dr. Hiroshi Inose, professor emeritus of the University of Tokyo, and Dr. Charles Kuen Kao, vice chancellor of the Chinese University of Hong Kong, whom I will mention in another chapter.

On October 18, 1988, the fourth C&C awards were given to Dr. Maurice V. Wilkes, former professor of the University of Cambridge, in the United Kingdom, and Dr. John S. Mayo, Mr. Eric E. Summer, and Mr. M. Robert Aaron, all of AT&T Bell Laboratories. It was most interesting that of the four recipients, one was selected for his pioneering contribution to the establishment of computer technology and the three AT&T researchers for their pioneering contribution to the development of digital communications technology. These two groups exactly covered C&C.

In addition to conferring these awards, the foundation also makes fellowship grants available to foreign researchers living in Japan to study at universities and public institutes in Japan. It also provides financial support to permit those researchers to present their papers at international conferences held outside Japan. It is my hope that I can make some small contribution to the diffusion of C&C through these activities.

SOFTWARE

"A computer without the software is just a box." This statement is often cited to show the importance of software, but although it has some validity, it is not entirely accurate. If we look back over the history of computers, software—in the sense of creative human intelligence—came first. If a sophisticated C&C system such as the one I have been advocating is ever to become user-friendly we will need to perfect this human/machine interface.

Around 1980 it occurred to me that by speaking only in terms of C&C I was leaving something out. One of our software engineers, Kiichi Fujino, said to me one day, "A thing doesn't become real until it is expressed three-dimensionally. To give your concept three-dimensionality, why don't you add 'man' as its third axis?" Surely no hardware specialist is likely to have come up with this idea. Since I believed that C&C needed the human touch, something that would make it seem more readily accessible, I changed the expression to "Man and C&C."

Never in my wildest dreams did I think that the addition of the word "man" would cause problems. But in April 1985, when I was asked to speak at Purdue University in Indiana, the president of the university came up to me with a concerned look on his face and said, "Mr. Kobayashi, forty percent of our students are women. If you call your talk 'Man and C&C,' they may regard the title as sexist and boycott your lecture. Would you please change the title to 'Humanity and C&C'?" "The word 'man' here is being used in the sense of 'humanity,' " I argued, "so I see no need to change it. But I understand your concern and will mention at the beginning of my speech that when I say 'man' I am referring to all human beings, women as well as men." My talk was a great success.

Some people predict that by the end of the twentieth century software costs will amount to as much as 90 percent of the cost of an entire computer system. Unless we can substantially reduce the cost of producing software, my dream of C&C will never be realized. Surely, I thought, there must be some way of streamlining software production? While I was pondering various approaches to the problem, the image of Mount Fuji suddenly came to mind. To climb Mount Fuji you can take a bus—or a car if you are in a hurry—as far as the fifth station, halfway up the mountain. But from there on, the ascent to the summit can be made only on foot. It struck me that the same was true of software. The production methods and management techniques used for the production of hardware could be applied to the production of the less demanding elements of software, which correspond to Mount Fuji below its fifth station. With this analogy in mind I gave orders to establish a Software Product Engineering Laboratory, which opened in July 1980 and has contributed greatly to the improvement of quality and productivity for what I like to refer to as "below-the-fifth-station" software.

Creating the right atmosphere is particularly important in translating an idea into reality. By "atmosphere" I mean an environment that will stimulate the mind to work. To create this atmosphere I provided opportunities for our software personnel to present reports on the results of our software quality-control campaign, popularly known as SWQC. The first papers were presented at a meeting in November 1981. Since then similar meetings have been held twice a year in the spring and fall. I always make it a point to attend.

Reflecting the decentralization that has epitomized my management philosophy is the construction of a nationwide software production map. Since the founding of NEC Software, in September 1975, we have sought to expand our software subsidiaries throughout the country. From Sapporo, Hokkaido, in the north, to Naha, Okinawa, in the south, we now have thirty two such companies, which are contributing to the revitalization of the local economy and helping communities make the shift away from heavy industries to services. Since software reflects language and customs and is thus suited by nature to local production, we are currently engaged in software development and production in the U.S. and several other countries. To prevent overlapping, our software products circulate around each of these production bases.

One of my goals is to perfect an automatic interpretation telephone. Such a telephone would automatically translate the words of someone speaking Japanese at one end of the line so that the party on the other end would hear the ideas in English, and vice versa. In 1983 NEC displayed a research model of such a device at the Telcom 83 exhibition, held in Geneva, Switzerland. The British actress who demonstrated the model performed with great enthusiasm, and after the exhibition she told me, with tears in her eyes, that she had never played a more meaningful role. Some years later, in October 1987, I was asked for the fourth time by the International Telecommunications Union to give the keynote address at Forum 87, which was held in conjuction with the Telecom 87 exhibition. After the opening ceremonies were over and I had some time to spare, I had dinner with the actress and some of her friends. I was able to tell her that the significance of that first demonstration had if anything grown with the arrival of recent developments. At the Telecom 87 exhibition, British Telecom displayed a model telephone for translating between English and French. I firmly believe that the day is steadily approaching when software and artificial-intelligence technology will be able to break down the language barriers that separate us.

ENTERING THE INFORMATION-SERVICES
BUSINESS

On April 1, 1985, the Nippon Telegraph and Telephone Public Corporation was privatized and reincarnated as the Nippon Telegraph and Telephone Company. With privatization came the complete deregulation of telecommunications services. The three laws governing the reform of Japan's telecommunications—the NTT Corporation Law, the Telecommunications Business Law, and the law on the enforcement of these two laws—went into effect on that day.

As with similar trends toward deregulation in the U.S., the world leader in information technology, Japan's piecemeal opening up of telecommunications services to the private sector, first in 1971 and then in 1982, was carried out in a way that confirmed how deeply computers had penetrated into the communications field. I found this particularly interesting because I could see the influence of my ideas on C&C behind these moves.

Back in 1969, when NEC was celebrating its seventieth anniversary, we had already been in the computer field for over ten years and had acquired considerable insight into what the computer business was all about. As a result of this experience I recognized the importance that information services would one day have as a business concern.

As I mentioned earlier, in September 1970 GE sold off its computer division to Honeywell. But it retained its information-services division and entrusted the management of this promising field to a subsidiary, GEISCO. I heard that software specialists within the company had advised GE's top management to keep their software and information-services division because it was certain to be a source of future livelihood.

Because I shared the same views and thought that a tie-up with a foreign company might be one way of expediting NEC's entry into the information-services field, I explored the possibilities of an affiliation with GE. I also spent some time trying to come to an agreement with Dentsu Incorporated, which was also in contact with GE at that time. In the end these talks fell through, and I decided we should enter the field on our own. At the beginning of

1971 I gave the go-ahead to proceed with laying the groundwork for this new business venture. NEC Information Services was founded in September 1974, with its main office in Tokyo. Sometime later GEISCO began to use new and powerful NEC mainframe computers for its information-services business.

Because the information environment of Japan was on the verge of changing from batch processing to on-line, at first we encountered many difficulties of one kind or another. But although I heard grumblings from some that they didn't understand what information services was all about, or that we didn't have enough personnel for it, everyone concerned cooperated with me in laying the foundations and developing the new business. Many years would pass before the concept of a value-added network (VAN) would finally take hold. The market is gradually expanding and coming to maturity, but as a business venture information services is an area that still needs careful nurturing.

No undertaking can materialize overnight. I have always believed that for a value-added network business to blossom, it is vitally important to have both a long-term perspective, one that looks ahead to the twenty-first century, and an efficient policy for investing the company's resources based on such long-term views.

The Commercialization of Fiber-Optic Communications

This is the age of optoelectronics. My first encounter with optics dates back to 1960. I was visiting Hughes Aircraft at the time, and Lawrence A. Hyland told me confidentially that a Hughes engineer named Theodore H. Maiman, using a ruby crystal, had succeeded in obtaining the world's first pulsed laser action. Hyland, though nominally vice president, was de facto president of Hughes and had been involved in the development of radar for the U.S. Army before the war. I took his words as a kind of warning. "Most important inventions take twenty years before they can be put to use, but lasers are different," he said. "They are so remarkable, it will be only a matter of a few years before they are in practical use. Hughes is already organizing for laser research, production, and sales."

The appearance of the world's first laser meant that it was now possible to artificially generate coherent light; that is, light in which the electromagnetic waves maintain a fixed phase relationship with each other. In the past radio waves had been developed to extremely high frequencies, known as millimeter waves, for use in communications; now the same thing could be done with light. I realized immediately that this was an enormously significant invention.

As soon as I returned home I had NEC begin research on lasers. In 1961 we succeeded in attaining pulse oscillation of a ruby laser. I then appointed Teiji Uchida, who had just returned from studying in France, to push ahead with research on laser technology. Through the concerted efforts of everyone concerned, Uchida and his team were able to solve the technical problems involved in the construction of fiber-optic communications systems by the late 1970s. In 1980 NEC established the Fiber-Optic Communications Development Division within its Transmission and Terminal Group. On July 10 of that year the Optoelectronic Industry and Technology Development Association was started under the auspices of the Ministry of International Trade and Industry. I was asked to serve as the association's first president.

At present NEC has built fiber-optic communications networks not only in Japan, but in Europe, North and South America, and the Middle East, and has established a reputation as the world's top manufacturer in the field. I have particularly vivid memories of two of these overseas projects.

The world's first optical circuit in practical use was Vista-Florida Telephone's fiber-optic communications system. Vista is a telephone company in the state of Florida that has Disney World within its service area. At the beginning of 1977 NEC's local salespeople got word that Vista was planning to build a new telecommunications system. Here was the perfect opportunity to create a showcase that would attract the attention of the whole world. I went to Florida and proposed to the president of Vista that the company install an optical system. The president, a former university professor, approved my suggestion. Vista's was the first fiber-optic communications system exported by NEC.

In the spring of 1979, during the Argentina Digital Symposium in Buenos Aires, Argentina's telecommunications administration announced plans to build a digital communications network for that city. The deadline for bids was October 1979. Because of the importance of the project, I put Senior (now Executive) Vice President Toshiro Kunihiro in charge and submitted a bid for a system using optical fiber cable produced by Sumitomo Electric Industries. We proposed a 140-megabit system—then the fastest in the world. During the late 1960s and early 1970s NEC had made a place for itself on the world microwave market by pushing up the technology to levels rival companies were unable to offer. Taking my cue from that example, I decided that once again we had to outdo the competition by offering the latest technology at reasonable prices.

The Buenos Aires project was the largest of its kind in the world, and for the Argentine telecommunications administration it was quite literally a matter of deadly seriousness. Rumors were flying that if the system failed, all those concerned would be shot and their bodies dumped into the Rio de la Plata. The project called for a simultaneous switchover to the new optical system for all 1.6 million subscribers of the old telephone network. It was an enormous—indeed an unprecedented—undertaking, and I won't deny that I too had a few anxious moments. But I visited the site and added my words of encouragement. In 1981 the new fiber-optic communications network successfully began providing telephone service, and the call-completion rate for Buenos Aires shot up dramatically. As we had hoped, the project had a favorable influence on the development of our overseas corporate strategy, and by the end of 1987 we had delivered optical systems to more than forty foreign countries.

Within Japan NEC cooperated extensively with the Nippon Telegraph and Telephone Public Corporation (currently Nippon Telegraph and Telephone Company) for a commercial fiber-optic communications system—from on-site testing of a one-hundred-megabit system at the beginning of 1978, to the completed installation of optical cable running the entire length of the Japanese archipelago in February 1985. Because the use of fiber-optic communication systems is expected to extend to local area networks

(LAN) and cable television, mass production of the optical devices that are at the heart of these systems has become essential.
NEC built an optical-device plant in Otsuki City, Yamanashi
Prefecture, near my old home village. The plant, the first in the
world for this purpose, went into production in 1986. It fits in
well with the plans of Komei Mochizuki, governor of Yamanashi, to create an advanced industrial development project,
dubbed Crystal Valley, in his prefecture.

On November 26, 1987, the Foundation for C&C Promotion,
which I referred to earlier, held its third C&C award ceremony
at the Hotel Okura in Tokyo. One of the recipients was Charles
Kuen Kao. In 1966 he had been the first to predict the development of low-loss optical fibers and had paved the way for
fiber-optic communications.

PIONEERS ON THE FRONTIERS
OF SPACE

ISAS News is the bulletin of the Ministry of Education's Institute
of Space and Astronautical Science (formerly the Institute of
Space and Aeronautical Science at the University of Tokyo). In
the November 1986 issue I had the opportunity to reminisce
about the early days of space development in Japan and about
how NEC first became involved in Japan's space program.

In 1955 professors Hideo Itokawa and Noboru Takagi of the
University of Tokyo conducted the test flight of a pencil rocket
nine inches long and less than three-quarters of an inch in diameter. Not long afterwards NEC received a request from Professor Takagi to develop a telemetering device for their next
effort, the Kappa rocket. That year NEC began research in the
area under the leadership of Masatsugu Kobayashi, director of
the Central Research Laboratories. Thus NEC's space development program began at the very dawn of Japan's exploration of
space.

In 1964 the Kagoshima Space Center was opened on the Osumi Peninsula at the southernmost tip of Kyushu Island. The
following year the Institute of Space and Aeronautical Science
began functioning at the University of Tokyo, and the Space
Activity Promotion Center was set up by the Japanese govern-

ment's Science and Technology Agency. Thus, just around the time I became president of NEC, the groundwork for space development in Japan had been laid, and all at once the program was starting to take shape.

In September 1966 the first Japanese attempt to launch an artificial satellite into space was made, using the Lambda rocket. Just before the launch someone had to make a statement to the press. Because I happened to be at the launching site, there was a suggestion that I do it, but in the end it was Professor Itokawa who held the news conference. "The probability for success is thirty percent," he told them, "and I have almost no expectation the launch will succeed." True to his prediction, that launch did indeed end in failure. Finally on February 11, 1970, Japan's first artificial satellite was launched successfully. It was called *Osumi* after the peninsula where the launch site was located. The NEC engineering team that had been in charge of its production was elated.

Taking our cue from this success, we established a new Space Development Laboratory within the company. In May 1970 we added an Artificial Satellite Section to it. This was probably the first time in Japanese industry that the words "artificial satellite" were used in a section name. The following June I was nominated to succeed Atsushi Oya as the president of the Japan Federation of Economic Organizations Space Activity Promotion Council.

From the *Osumi* in 1970 to the *Akebono* in 1989, one new NEC-produced scientific satellite after another has gone into orbit. As of February 1989 the Ministry of Education's Institute of Space and Astronautical Science has launched eighteen artificial satellites or artificial planets, and NEC has been responsible for overseeing the production of them all. That is an accomplishment in which I take very great pride.

The mandate to develop an application satellite was entrusted to Japan's National Space Development Agency (NASDA), which started operations in October 1969. NASDA's very first artificial satellite, the *Kiku*, was also produced under NEC supervision. Planning soon began in earnest for the development of weather, communications, and broadcasting satellites. This touched off the trade wars in the latter half of the 1970s over who would build Japan's first weather satellite. To our good fortune NEC received the order. In July 1977 Japan's first application satellite, the weather satellite *Himawari*, was launched from Cape Canaveral in the U.S. NEC has also been responsible for Japan's other two weather satellites, *Himawari 2* and *Himawari 3*. These satellites have brought the frontiers of space into Japanese living rooms via television weather broadcasts, and their names have become household words.

In 1982 I addressed the American Association for the Advancement of Science at its meeting in Washington, D.C. In my speech, entitled "The Impact of Space Technology and C&C," I stressed that the development of space technology was indispensable for the healthy development of international society. At an international conference held that March at Leeds Castle in Kent, England, I saw with my own eyes the discord between the industrialized and Third World countries over space development and vowed to do my best to eliminate the gap between the North and South in the area of telecommunications services.

The advances made by NEC in space development have proceeded at a rapid rate. The success of the marine observation satellite *Momo 1;* the progress in research on a space station; the successful experiments by the Asahi Shimbun in the crystallization of artificial snow and the impact of a steel ball on water drops, both of which employed NEC equipment and made use of the special environmental conditions of outer space—developments in this area have indeed been dizzyingly fast.

In February 1986 the Japan Space Utilization Promotion Center was founded to support research in new materials and biotechnology that will take advantage of the minimal gravity of outer space. I was asked to be president. That June I resigned the presidency of the Space Activity Promotion Council, which I had held for fifteen years. Tadahiro Sekimoto, president of NEC, was chosen to succeed me.

RESEARCH AND DEVELOPMENT

On December 23, 1987, I was standing on the site of Tsukuba EXPO '85, Japan's highly successful scientific world fair, for the ground-breaking ceremonies of NEC's new Tsukuba Laboratories.

With Dr. L. A. Hyland, vice president of the Hughes Aircraft Company, at a Hughes plant. At the back is an Intelsat IV-series communications satellite.

As a keynote speaker at the Intelcom 77 in Atlanta, Georgia, October 1977. Here I advocated the C&C concept publicly for the first time.

The family, 1961.

*Speaking to Harvard Business School
professors and students, December 1982.*

*Telecom 83, Geneva, seated before the
demonstrators of NEC's automatic
interpretation telephone.*

Receiving the key to the City of San Francisco from Mayor Dianne Feinstein, 1984. After NEC's automatic fingerprint-identification system was installed by the city's police department, there was a significant decrease in burglaries.

*The NEC Semiconductors (UK) plant in
Livingston, Scotland, was formally opened by
Her Majesty Queen Elizabeth II on July 4,
1983.*

*The first C&C Awards presentation ceremony
by the Foundation for C&C Promotion, Tokyo,
November 1985.*

Welcoming His Majesty the Crown Prince Akihito (now His Majesty the Emperor of Japan) at NEC Central Research Laboratories, May 9, 1985.

Receiving an honorary membership of the National Institute for Higher Education in Dublin, Ireland, 1986.

Receiving the Special UN Medal of Peace for
International Law Enforcement Cooperation,
April 1986.

My wife and three daughters celebrate my receiving the Grand Cordon of the Order of the Rising Sun from His Majesty the Emperor of Japan, November 3, 1987.

NEC has traditionally prided itself on its commitment to technological progress. Over the years we have stressed the importance of R&D and have committed many of our most capable personnel to this sector. After I became president in 1964 I threw my energy behind efforts to improve the efficiency of our R&D organization, strengthen and perfect our technology-development strategy, and develop original and independent technologies. These efforts have paid off. I once had a survey taken of the percentage of NEC's total annual sales accounted for by products that had been developed within the previous five years. The average was around 70 percent for the company as a whole, and exceeded 90 percent for some divisions.

The basic idea behind research and development at NEC is what I like to refer to as "divergence and convergence." By "divergence" I mean dispersing responsibility for R&D throughout the entire company and creating organizational units where research activities are closely connected with business performance. Because these decentralized research activities are more concentrated and thus much easier to direct, this is where the idea of "convergence" enters in.

Based on this R&D strategy, NEC set up a three-tiered decentralized system of research and development activity. An R&D group does not belong to central corporate staff; it is placed as a functional unit among line operating groups, each of which comprises several divisions. Each division acts as a profit center for its own business operations. It has direct ties with the marketplace and, in order to ensure its profits, must develop products that the market wants. Because management at the division level is most sensitive to current market needs, it has the responsibility for developing technology for "today." The development division of an operating group has the responsibility for R&D into technology for "tomorrow," for nurturing the seeds of what will eventually grow into new business ventures. Only the group responsible for research and development for the "day after tomorrow" is referred to at NEC as its R&D group. Because this group is not much swayed by current market needs, its duties range from basic research into technologies that will be important for the future, to applied research and basic development, right down to leading-edge research into the basic technologies needed to establish or revise corporate strategy. I have divided R&D into these three tiers but have made them interrelated. That is my philosophy of research and development guidance.

In one corner of the Tama Hills in Kawasaki City are located the NEC Central Research Laboratories. Originally our Central Research Laboratories had been on the site of the Tamagawa plant, but these labs had begun to show their age. To modernize and enhance our R&D facilities we built new laboratories on a fourteen-acre site with almost four hundred thousand square feet of building space.

Right after the ground-breaking ceremonies in 1973 came the first oil shock. Although we faced both a recession and difficulties in obtaining the materials we needed, we managed to overcome these problems and open the new labs. Construction was completed in the spring of 1975 and the opening ceremony was held that July.

In July 1980 NEC began a major organizational reform of its R&D system, the first such reshuffling since May 1965. My proposal for the integration of computers and communications had taken hold in industries throughout the world, and market needs were beginning to reflect this trend toward C&C. To better accommodate R&D plans to business strategies, I decided to decentralize our research activities even further as a means of enhancing our maneuverability.

The various laboratories that had belonged to our Central Research Laboratories were consolidated or reorganized, and five independent labs were created: the Basic Technologies Research Laboratories, the Optoelectronics Research Laboratories, the C&C Systems Research Laboratories, the Software Product Engineering Laboratory, and the Resources and Environment Protection Research Laboratories. In June 1982 the Basic Technologies Research Laboratories were divided into the Fundamental Research Laboratories and the Microelectronics Research Laboratories. In July 1986 the C&C Systems Research Laboratories were reinforced by the C&C Information Technology Research Laboratories. The Software Product Engineering Laboratory was absorbed into the newly founded Software Development Group in September 1987. These changes give some indication of the way NEC has poured its energies into strengthening its software capabilities.

It takes at least twenty years for an invention that shows promise of a technological breakthrough to develop into a technology with a firm enough footing to become a viable commercial venture. A good example of this is satellite communications. In a 1945 radio magazine article British science-fiction writer Arthur C. Clarke proposed the launching of three satellites 22,300 miles above the equator from which television broadcasts could be beamed throughout the world. Twenty years later Harold A. Rosen of Hughes Aircraft was able to translate this idea into reality. As I discussed in an earlier chapter, NEC cooperated with Hughes from the very beginning of that project. If this rule of thumb continues to apply, we will have to start envisioning today the technology that will be needed twenty years from now.

The NEC C&C Hall of Technological History was opened in February 1985. In this exhibition hall are displayed the achievements of the world's pioneers in computers and communications—such as Yasujiro Niwa and Akira Nakashima, who sparked the technological innovations at NEC in the 1930s; Jack A. Morton of Bell Laboratories; and Lawrence A. Hyland of Hughes Aircraft. The exhibits also trace the technological development of each of NEC's business areas. My steps have brought me back many times to this exhibition hall.

An International Corporation

It is only natural for someone facing an important event to be nervous. It was a long, exciting day for me. Our British subsidiary, NEC Semiconductors (UK), was holding the opening ceremonies for its newly completed semiconductor plant in Livingston, Scotland, to which Her Majesty Queen Elizabeth II had been invited. The queen was greeted by the marquess of Linlithgow, who presented my wife and me to her, after which I introduced the other representatives of NEC. At the site of the ceremonies the queen pulled open a curtain to reveal a plaque with the inscription: "This factory was opened by Her Majesty the Queen on the fourth of July, 1983."

Two days after that festive occasion, I was in London visiting Prime Minister Margaret Thatcher at 10 Downing Street. "If NEC's semiconductor plant in Scotland will contribute to the prosperity of British industry," I told her, "I won't mind if it becomes a British factory. Please regard it as your own child." Mrs. Thatcher readily consented to my request. One year later I had a second audience with the queen at a garden party at Buckingham Palace. "This is an LSI made at our plant in Scotland," I said and handed Her Majesty a semiconductor chip, which the queen accepted with a smile. I was genuinely and deeply moved.

NEC Semiconductors (UK) had been founded in June 1981 and began producing LSIs in October of the following year. It was NEC's twentieth overseas plant, yet another embodiment of my views that our operations should be dispersed not only throughout Japan but throughout the world. In October 1987 the plant began production of a state-of-the-art semiconductor device, the one-megabit dynamic RAM. This British-made LSI will undoubtedly be exported not only to the rest of Europe but even to the United States. A business that transcends national borders has formally begun.

NEC's second plant in the United Kingdom was the NEC Technologies (UK) plant at Priorslee, Telford, which was officially opened on November 2, 1988, by Her Royal Highness the Princess of Wales. The opening ceremony, hosted by me, was attended by about three hundred local dignitaries and guests as well as NEC people from Japan. This plant manufactures video-cassette recorders, computer printers, mobile telephones, and facsimile machines, some 70 percent being for export to continental European countries.

NEC's first European semiconductor plant was opened in the Republic of Ireland in October 1976. When I went to Ireland in 1986 to attend its tenth-anniversary celebrations, government officials and the local people gave me a gala welcome. On that occasion I was awarded an honorary membership from the National Institute for Higher Education in Dublin.

In the United States we purchased Electronic Arrays, located in Mountain View, California, and set up a production base there. Although it provided us with useful lessons in American-style management methods, our sacrifice in profits was substantial. The equipment was outmoded and unsuited to producing ultra-modern microelectronics devices. We decided to build a new through-process plant for VLSIs in Roseville, California. The opening ceremonies were held in October 1985. That year the controversy between the U.S. and Japan over semiconductors had flared up again, so we were concerned about what sort of reception we would be given there. Fortunately we were welcomed.

Closer to home I visited Beijing in November 1975 as the leader of a friendship mission representing Japan's electronics industry. This was my second visit to the People's Republic of China since the end of World War II. I remember suggesting to Zhong Fuxiang, director-general of posts and telecommunications, and other officials whom we met that, in view of China's vast size, they first consider building a microwave system to provide the necessary communications infrastructure. Just as ancient Chinese civilization had once developed along the banks of the Yellow River where fertile farmlands had been brought under cultivation, people had settled, and fortified towns had sprung up, so today China's modernization would evolve along the routes of its information and communications network.

Some time was needed for these ideas to germinate, but around 1978 plans for a microwave communications system began to take shape. The project started with the Beijing-Wuhan route, which was completed in 1979, then work began on the Beijing-Shanghai and the Hainan Island-Guangzhou routes. In the end NEC was in charge of building a microwave network that extended nearly 7,700 miles.

In the summer of 1985 I had the opportunity to attend the cutover ceremony for digital switching systems NEC supplied to the Tianjin Posts and Telecommunications Administration. NEC later helped to open nearly one hundred telephone offices there. I was grateful to the Chinese authorities for their confidence in us and at the same time deeply aware that none of this would have been possible without the efforts of all concerned at NEC.

The China-Japan Software Center was set up in Beijing in January 1982. As I recall, back in November 1979 about the time that NEC had just finished coping with the second OPEC oil shock, I broached the subject of setting up a software center to Vice Premier Wan Zhen (now vice president of the People's Republic of China) during a friendly discussion about advances in the information revolution. The vice premier agreed to supply the building if NEC provided the computers and the technicians for them. Since then more than fifteen hundred Chinese have trained at the center. As is widely known, many Chinese are actively engaged in the computer industry throughout the world. It is my fondest wish that the training they receive at the China-Japan Software Center will help many more talented young people to develop their abilities to the full.

Today NEC does business with 145 countries throughout the world. It has 57 locally incorporated companies and twenty-five plants in twenty-four different countries. The total number of NEC employees outside Japan is nineteen thousand people, only 3 percent of whom are Japanese. Each year as many as seven thousand employees travel abroad on official business. NEC has become an international corporation.

I began to think that overseas operations would be an important corporate strategy in 1974. In my New Year's address I designated 1974 as the year to "go global" and begin large-scale development. Through competition with the leading companies of the world we have been able to upgrade our technology, streamline production, and step up sales. By honing our skills in the international marketplace, we learned through on-the-job training just what it is that foreign markets want. NEC's international growth has given me tremendous personal satisfaction.

My first business trip abroad dates back to 1937. Since then I have traveled overseas nearly two hundred times and have made many foreign friends. I have enjoyed a long association with Lawrence A. Hyland of Hughes Aircraft and have learned greatly from his almost visionary insight. I have known Charles L. Brown, former chairman of the board at AT&T, for more than twenty years. And of course I have maintained a close friendship with Jerome B. Wiesner, president emeritus of the Massachusetts Institute of Technology. Every year I send out more than two thousand Christmas cards, and I always enjoy writing them, recalling familiar faces and voices as I sign each card.

I have always believed that the basis of a successful international strategy boils down to six points:

1. International operations require time.
2. The simplistic view "If the domestic market is bad, go international" does not make sense.

3. Have your production and marketing facilities as close to your market as possible.
4. Take full advantage of local management resources.
5. Maintain a well-balanced global distribution of production facilities.
6. Top management must have a clear vision of international management principles and trends.

Time does indeed fly. Some of the subsidiaries NEC has established throughout the world are beginning to celebrate the tenth anniversary of their founding; a few are even in their twentieth year of operation. In June 1987, when one of our computer companies outside Boston held its tenth-anniversary party, the American president addressed me as "my father." I was deeply affected.

THE AUTOMATIC
FINGERPRINT-IDENTIFICATION SYSTEM

Computer-based research into pattern recognition began to pick up in the mid-1960s. Tests were made of the computer's ability to recognize letters, patterns, and sounds. At NEC's Central Research Laboratories R&D in this area moved ahead under the direction of Kazuo Kiji. These efforts bore fruit, and around 1968 the National Police Agency of Japan enquired about the possibility of our developing a system for automatically identifying fingerprints. We immediately initiated research on the project, and in 1982 we delivered the first automatic fingerprint-identification system to the National Police Agency. This system is not an imitation of European or American technology. It is the product of original Japanese research and development and far more sophisticated than similar systems produced in other countries. Since it has been in operation it has solved a number of important cases.

The NEC system has attracted the attention of police agencies abroad, especially in the United States. The San Francisco City Police Department installed the very first fingerprint-identification system we exported. In March 1984 I happened to be in San Francisco to attend an international conference. While I was at a conference session I received a message from the mayor of San Francisco, Dianne Feinstein, asking me to come to city hall to receive the key to the city.

On March 15 I visited the mayor's office, where Mayor Feinstein and Chief of Police Cornelius Murphy were waiting for me. After reviewing what the NEC automatic fingerprint-identification system had accomplished during its first two weeks of operation, the mayor congratulated me and handed me the key to the city. Then, with evident pride, she explained that when she was in Japan she had learned that the National Police Agency of Japan had installed a very effective system, whereupon she had immediately relayed this information to the San Francisco Police Department. In the three years since the system was introduced, the number of burglaries in San Francisco has dropped 24 percent. Few businessmen are lucky enough to play a part in a commercial venture of such unequivocal benefit to society.

Since then the NEC system has been delivered to major police agencies not only within Japan and the United States but also in Canada, Australia, and Spain. In April 1986 I was awarded the Special United Nations Medal of Peace for International Law-Enforcement Cooperation by one of the UN's nongovernment organizations. The reason given for the award was that through the development and delivery of an automatic fingerprint-identification system I had contributed to the maintenance of civic peace. I shall always remember the scene of the award ceremony at the main conference room of the UN headquarters in New York City.

A Sense of Mission and My "Ten Pointers for Executives"

"A stable company is unstable; an unstable one is stable." I shall never forget hearing those words at a seminar given by an American lecturer right after the war. A company that realizes it is unstable will do its utmost to achieve stability. A stable company, on the other hand, becomes unstable through its attempts to preserve the status quo.

Just like a person a company has its own appointed lifespan. Even many first-rate companies have begun to go downhill after they reach sixty or thereabouts. Although NEC was founded in 1899, it did not begin to grow as an independent company until around 1960. I like to think of NEC as a company in its thirties just entering its prime, for whom complacency is still anathema.

When I became president in 1964 NEC's sales were 80 billion yen; in 1988 they were 2.7 trillion yen. In a period of twenty-four years they increased thirty-three-fold. Perhaps growth such as we have known will be impossible in the future. I keep telling my staff over and over again: "Never think in terms of continuing along the same lines that have gone before."

How does NEC rank in the world today with respect to sales? It is fourth in communications equipment, fifth in computers, and first in semiconductors. No other company the whole world over possesses such a good balance of the three business areas that will form the basis for the advanced information society of tomorrow.

Some difficult tasks lie ahead for us, however. One of our business areas is home electronics. Here, quite frankly, I cannot say we have achieved success. The area was dear to the heart of my predecessor, the late Toshihide Watanabe, and he entrusted it to my care. I changed the original concept and, under the guise of bringing C&C into the home, established it as one of the mainstays of our corporate strategy. We also started using the expression "home electronics" instead of "electrical appliances."

In 1983 I embarked on a restructuring and changed the name of the company in charge of our home electronics line from New Nippon Electric Company to NEC Home Electronics. I firmly believe that in the course of time home electronics will become one of the four mainstays of NEC, along with communications, computers, and semiconductors.

Back in 1970, when I was visiting Paraguay in South America, I was told that because Paraguay was surrounded on all sides by other countries, more than anything else it wanted an eye of its own through which to look directly at the world. This was the way the government of Paraguay expressed their president's wish to have a satellite-communications earth station.

I resolved to fulfill the president's request. We used our good offices to arrange yen credit for Paraguay to help finance the earth station. When it was finally built, everyone was delighted, and perhaps for that reason I was awarded the Orden Nacional del Mérito with the rank of *comendador* from the government of the Republic of Paraguay in 1978. I have also received honors from Peru (the Grand Cross); Jordan (the Jordan Star); Egypt (the Order of Merit of the First Grade); Brazil (the National Order of the Southern Cross); Poland (the Commander's Cross of the Order of Merit); Thailand (the Order of the White Elephant); Madagascar (Chevalier du Mérite); Colombia (Order of San Carlos); and Spain (Encomienda en la Orden del Mérito Civil).

The majority of these honors have been for our contribution to the upgrading of these countries' telecommunications networks, and show how fervently all countries desire to perfect the telecommunications sector of their social infrastructure. I feel I have a mission to help them achieve this goal that transcends any purely business considerations.

On November 3, 1987, Culture Day in Japan, two days after these jottings began to be serialized in the *Nihon Keizai Shimbun*, I quite unexpectedly received the Grand Cordon of the Order of the Rising Sun from his majesty the emperor of Japan. I feel I was commended for having lived long and worked hard. I am filled with deep emotion at receiving this honor far greater than I deserved.

I have many pleasant memories of my contacts with institutions of higher learning all over the world. At Harvard Business School Professor Michael E. Porter used my C&C corporate strategy as the theme of a case study. Professor Porter praised my work, saying that from the skillful blending of the mutually related business areas of computers and communications had been created "one of the few large diversified companies where the whole really adds up to more than the subparts." One of the results of this study was to draw worldwide attention to NEC's management strategies and the results they had attained.

I have received four honorary doctorates: from Monmouth College (Illinois) and the Polytechnic Institute of Brooklyn (New York); from the Autonomous University of Guadalajara, Mexico; and from the University of the Philippines. I received an honorary membership from the National Institute for Higher Education in Ireland and also a presidential citation for meritorious services from New York University.

The major national honors I have received in Japan are the Grand Cordon of the Order of the Rising Sun, the First Class Order of the Sacred Treasure, the Purple Ribbon Medal, and the Blue Ribbon Medal. Awards from learned societies include the Frederik Philips Award and the Founders Medal from the Institute of Electrical and Electronics Engineers (IEEE); the Distinguished Service Award from both the Institute of Electrical Communication Engineers of Japan and the Information Processing Society of Japan; the Distinguished Achievement Award from the Operations Research Society; the Japanese Broadcasting Culture Award from NHK; and the Management Sciences Prize for Merit from the Japan Management Association. The most recent honor I have received is the Hall of Fame award given on April 5, 1989, by the Washington, D.C.–based Society of Satellite Professionals International in recognition of my efforts in the development of satellite communications.

I am deeply fortunate to have been blessed with such kind mentors, colleagues, friends, and acquaintances, through whose help and encouragement I have been able to pursue my work without encountering any serious setbacks. My wife, who is the mainstay of my existence, is in good health and continues to show me her unstinting understanding and forbearance. My three daughters are happily married, and my seven grandchildren are all well and attending school.

In my 1982 book *C&C and Software* I published some of the ideas I had noted down for my own reference or had passed on to others under the heading "Ten Pointers for Executives." In the hope that these ideas may serve as guidelines to the next generation, I reprint them here.

1. Make a picture of your thoughts. Maps and sketches are an invaluable guide in attaining your objectives.
2. To grasp the situation in which you find yourself, take account of a coordinate axis of both time and space.
3. Recognize that a seemingly stable corporation contains elements of instability, while a seemingly unstable corporation can be stable.
4. Teamwork multiplies individual abilities. Don't forget the proverb "Two heads are better than one."
5. Do not follow a one–way, single track in your thinking.

Set up feedback loops as a means of rectifying your own one-sided judgments.

6. In any undertaking, things develop from points to lines, and from lines to dimensions. Keep in mind, for example, that marketing and technology form a matrix.

7. Divergence versus convergence, the parts versus the whole—consider the advantages and disadvantages of both sides and always cultivate a sense of balance.

8. Do not be swamped by the rising tide of information and knowledge. Be selective. Remember that the most important information is not always the most visible.

9. Self-help is the mainstay of development for both the individual and society.

10. Cultivate the strong points and potentials of an individual or an enterprise and nurture them like a gardener. They may take ten or twenty years to mature.

When I walk across from my office to an open space on the twenty-second floor of the NEC Building, I can see from a window the entire expanse of a construction site one block away. This is the site of NEC's new corporate headquarters, which will be completed in 1989, the ninetieth anniversary of the company's founding. It will be an intelligent building, built in anticipation of the information society of the twenty-first century. No doubt our new high-rise headquarters, forty-three stories high with four stories underground, will be an imposing sight in the Tokyo skyline.

APPENDIX

NEC'S MANAGEMENT AND ITS C&C STRATEGY

Author's Note:
The following is an address I delivered to professors, students, and guests of Harvard University's Graduate School of Business Administration on December 6, 1982. In it I attempted to give a clear view of my C&C concept and to explain what I believe to be the role of a CEO in any business enterprise. The occasion also allowed me to summarize my own management goals and to trace the paths I followed in reaching them. I am grateful to have had the opportunity to express myself in this fashion before such a distinguished audience.

CONTENTS

1. Introduction: Case Study of NEC Management

Ladies and gentlemen, as you are undoubtedly aware, a descriptive study of NEC management has been chosen for inclusion in the management case studies of this prestigious business school. I am therefore deeply honored to have been invited here today and to have this opportunity of speaking to you about NEC's management and its C&C strategy.

In the atmosphere of deepening stagflation that has emerged in the wake of the oil crises, growing attention has focused on Japanese-style management since the late 1970s. Published works by two intellectual soulmates of mine with very close links to Boston are deeply associated with this trend. One of these is Dr. James Abegglen's *The Japanese Factory*, published in the late 1950s, and the other the more recent *Japan as No. 1*, by Professor Ezra Vogel, which came out at the end of the 1970s.

Theory Z, by Professor Ouchi of UCLA; *The Art of Japanese Management*, coauthored by Professor Anthony G. Athos of Harvard University and Professor Richard T. Pascale of Stanford University; and a number of other books on the subject have also become best-sellers. Japanese-style management has been hailed as a possible solution to the present dilemma facing management, and a flood of delegations from abroad have come to Japan to observe Japanese enterprises. Personally, though, I discern a discrepancy between the picture these companies are painting of themselves and the picture painted by those who come to observe them. At NEC, I have warned employees not to jump on the bandwagon and start boasting about Japanese-style management.

What impresses me about the NEC management case study prepared by Harvard is that it avoids the pitfall of stereotyped preconceptions of Japanese-style management and presents a factual description of the way things actually are. In addition, the study does not stop at being a teaching text in business management, but also provides a most valuable reference work for overseas businessmen trying to understand Japan.

From my own knowledge of Japanese and American companies I see both similarities and differences. There are areas of strength and weakness on both sides. I would be very happy if you would bear this premise in mind in listening to the rest of my talk.

2. The CEO's Role as Captain of the Corporate Ship: Steering the Company

There exist a number of cultural differences between Japan and America; there are also differences in business management.

It is said that the foremost role of the chief executive officer in America is that of decision-maker. However, there are virtually no words that correspond well to this term in the Japanese vocabulary of management. Rather, I prefer the term *steering* as a description of the chief executive's prime responsibility. That is, I believe steering the company is the most important job of the person serving as captain of the corporate ship. Keeping his bearings on a lighthouse in the dark of night, maintaining his course in defiance of angry seas, guiding his ship safely through uncharted waters . . . These are the responsibilities of the chief executive as the captain of his company. As the first topic of my speech today I wish to talk about this kind of responsibility.

Functioning as such a captain in my capacity as chief executive officer of Nippon Electric Company (NEC), I have had three major experiences with charting new courses for my company.

The first, some seventeen years ago, consisted of defining the course that NEC should follow in the postwar development of electronics. *Electronics* is a technical term that connotes a fantastic variety of potential applications. The resources of a single company, however, are limited, and each company must determine certain specific areas within which to operate.

Thus I set a course for NEC by which the company would specialize in areas concerned with the handling of information. In part I am indebted to America for the inspiration behind this idea. I am referring to the inspiration provided by Professor Fritz Machlup of Princeton University in his book *The Production and Distribution of Knowledge in the United States.*

After careful deliberation I decided to steer NEC toward a concentration on such major fields as communications for information transmission and computers for information processing—and of course semiconductors as the key components for them.

Consequently, I closed the Nuclear Energy Research Laboratory, which had been established in expectation of the appearance of some new fields of business for NEC in atomic energy.

The main thing suggested to me by the ideas of Professor Machlup was that the production of knowledge and information would likely prove to have much greater potential for future economic development than physical production. Around the time I was becoming interested in his ideas, I was also stimulated by the views on postindustrial society expressed by Professor Daniel Bell, then of Columbia University. Professor Bell's books kindled in me an interest in the transformation of industrial society as a whole.

I was not exposing myself only to the thinking of American scholars, however. I was also impressed by the "information industry" concept argued by Japan's Professor Tadao Umesao, and worked to integrate his ideas with those of the Americans and others from a business standpoint.

This sort of perspective was not unique to NEC but took hold throughout modern industry as a general awareness that such a path ought to be followed. This cognizance culminated in the adoption of the slogan "Toward knowledge-intensive industry," as part of the Japanese government's industrial policy in the 1970s. The fact that the course I had charted for the company under my own management was in line with the trends prevailing in industrial society at large further convinced me that I had indeed been on the mark.

3. The Establishment of a Corporate Identity

In the 1970s the prevailing mood of growth and development changed completely. Environmental problems, consumer and community campaigns against traditional industry, and shifts in the international monetary system combined to present serious and pressing problems for manufacturers everywhere.

In April 1971 the Club of Rome held its second world conference in Montebello, the same Ottawa suburb where the seventh summit of the seven leading industrialized countries was held. It elucidated mankind's potentially catastrophic situation as detailed in the work *The Limits to Growth*. In October of the same year, I was invited to the Innovation Group Conference held at Harrison House in the New York suburb of Glen Cove on Long Island. The discussion centered on two formal topics. One was the "Zero-Growth Economy." I think the ideas expounded in Lester C. Thurow's book *The Zero-Sum Society*, currently the subject of much attention, are not unrelated to the lively debate that took place there. My ideas also were solicited, and I offered the example of Japan's historical experience with zero economic growth and zero population growth during the approximately 250 years from the end of the sixteenth century to the midnineteenth century.

The other formal topic of discussion and debate at the conference was "The Crisis of Corporate Identity." In connection with this topic there was a panel discussion on the theme "How Three Bellwether Firms Are Shaping Themselves for the Future." Just as there is no Japanese term that corresponds well to *decision-making*, neither is there any suitable Japanese term for the word *identity*. However, the idea of a company without an identity is like that of a man without a soul—thus it can hardly be said that there is no such thing as corporate identity in Japanese business. This sort of language barrier cannot be overcome easily, and after much agonizing I finally hit on a plan: I would show NEC's business in a single picture. This picture is now being used as a representation of the NEC company tree, as shown in Figure 1.

These discussions at the Innovation Group Conference proved very useful to me. I came to realize that with human society undergoing profound change and all countries—including the

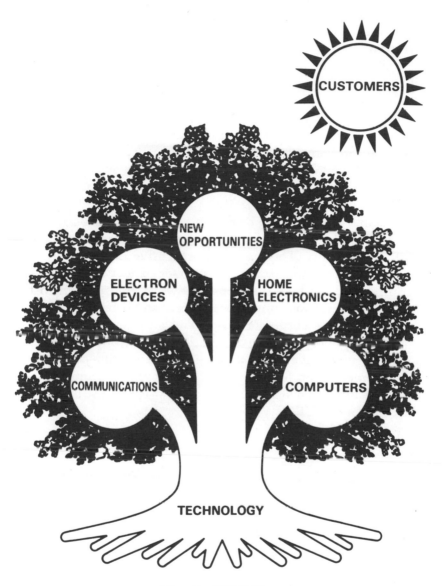

Fig. 1 NEC Tree

United States, which had led in every field until the end of the 1960s—faced with new problems and challenges, the nations of the world had reached a point where status considerations were irrelevant.

Following the bright 1960s, the somber 1970s were a period of simultaneous worldwide stagflation. Those of us in Japanese business worked unceasingly to cope with the difficulties confronting us. A few specific examples of steps that were taken include pollution-control measures; energy and resource conservation; improvements in product performance, quality, and reliability; the establishment of a dialogue with society at large; and the general improvement and streamlining of company organization.

Seeking to harmonize company activities with social development, I formulated and implemented a new program I called Operation Quality. This was a comprehensive approach intended to improve quality in seven areas: management capability and performance, products and services, work environment, local community relations, employee attitudes and behavior, business achievement, and corporate image. This program was essentially a "survival policy" for the perpetuation of the company. A management perspective based on such "quality of life" considerations seemed to be fundamental to the working approach of a chief executive. This essentially was my second act in steering the company as CEO.

4. Orienting NEC's Business to C&C

The 1970s have been appropriately likened to a long dark tunnel, as we crept along at the bottom of Kondrativ's theoretical fifty-year business cycle. I was not satisfied, however, with what people were calling a response to "slow growth." I asserted that what we really ought to aim for was "stable growth."

With the emergence of the Japanese economy from the tunnel in the 1980s, we looked around and were startled to discover the international economic position we had attained. Only a few other countries had been able, like Japan, to somehow weather the two oil crises relatively unscathed. The resilience, adaptability, and vitality of the Japanese economy became the focus of worldwide attention.

This performance of the overall Japanese economy is itself worthy of study. But when we limit our consideration to the electronic industry and to our company in particular, we find that something was beginning, like fresh magma, to take form. This was nothing other than the progress in semiconductor devices and integrated circuits (ICs).

Seventeen years ago, when I was giving a great deal of thought to the notion of a knowledge industry, we at NEC were in the process of making an important decision. One decisive action taken at the time was to make substantial investments in the semiconductor industry. By that time transistors had already developed into ICs and later into large-scale integration (LSIs). They have recently approached the mega-bit order of very large-scale integration (VLSIs). We perceived that this and other developments were bringing about major changes in the field of telecommunications and computers. This gave a fresh impetus to the development of digitalization, which was already under way in the area of communications.

My understanding at the time was that this digitalization of communications would mean the increased homogeneity of telecommunications technology and computer technology.

With regard to computers, it was becoming increasingly clear that there would be more value in pursuing an improvement of efficiency through distributed processing architecture than in simply building huge centralized computers. "Multipolar decentralization" means that several computers are linked together in a constellation-like structure through communications networks.

Seeking a single phrase to express both halves of this integration, I hit on the term C&C, short for "the integration of computers and communications. Needless to say, advances in semiconductor ICs were the technological key to achieving this integration, as shown in Figure 2. I presented my ideas on this subject at the Intelcom '77 conference held in Atlanta in October 1977.

The significance of C&C can be epitomized in the following three points.

1. C&C will form the framework of the system that will

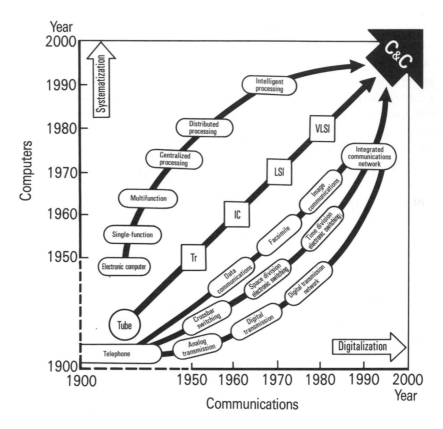

Fig. 2 A Perspective of C&C

hereafter function as the world's information-related infrastructure.

2. With information being handled more and more as a resource, this infrastructure will be a valuable tool for achieving economic and cultural development through the exchange and utilization of information.

3. The effective use of information resources will actually contribute to the development and efficient use of the physical resources—including energy and food—that are currently under heavy constraints.

In C&C I found the path for NEC to follow. This was of great significance in coordinating the activities of employees in all areas of the company, and in facilitating effective responses to the needs of every strata of customer; in other words, effecting a consolidation of the corporate identity.

Plotting this course for NEC was my third major act in steering the company as chief executive.

5. Seeking NEC's Position in the World

At first glance it may seem strange that I introduced my concept of C&C not in Tokyo, where our company headquarters is located, but in Atlanta. One reason was that the economic environment in Japan was not at all favorable to the formation of this kind of idea. Another reason perhaps was that communications is something one can only truly grasp after first getting out into the world and obtaining a global perspective. With our market encompassing more than 140 countries, we were already carrying out operations throughout the world as we worked with satellite and microwave communications, fiber-optic communications, switching systems, and every other sort of equipment for handling information. It was this, I believe, that made it possible for me to see the inevitability and neccessity of a new path of development for C&C.

Today NEC has production bases in twelve countries, and one-third of our production goes to meeting the demands of overseas markets. Things have reached a point where each year our young employees make a total of more than six thousand trips abroad and NEC in Tokyo welcomes over one thousand engineers and technicians from overseas customers in return.

In this way our operations have spread around the globe. At the same time, however, we felt it essential that we take steps to prevent this expansion from being seen as a Japanese invasion that might become a source of economic friction. I am delighted to say that, as a result of having proceeded cautiously and of having sought to assure host countries that there would be ample mutual benefits wherever we were invited and welcomed, no friction has yet arisen. Our manufacturing operations in Australia, Brazil, Malaysia, the United Kingdom, the United States and other countries have been set up as wholly owned or joint-venture companies with the express welcome of the host country.

In the light of the international nature of these ventures, and in response to actual developments in internationalization, I have taken every opportunity to express my opinion on C&C, not only in Japan but throughout the world. Sometimes I have focused on telecommunications, at other times on computers. On some occasions I have shifted my attention to software and the place of man in the C&C concept.

From the time I returned from the 1977 Atlanta conference, where I announced the C&C concept, to the early part of 1978, I used every opportunity to gather key management at the company guest house and hold what one might call fireside discussions on the possible future of C&C. These meetings were the forerunner of the C&C Committeee I launched in June 1978.

I also took a flexible approach to reorganizing and gearing company organization to accommodate C&C. This is reflected in the establishment of the Software Product Engineering Laboratory, the Personal Computer Division, the Robotics Division, and other reforms.

In addition to this I issued the following appeal to our staff at NEC, urging them to thoroughly familiarize themselves with our products: "A thorough understanding of, and ability to use, computers is the first step toward C&C. This will serve as a means of realizing the importance of software."

This is how I set about establishing the concept of C&C together with the appropriate company structures and got the company moving in that direction.

Following the course I set as chief executive, we began to orient ourselves toward the knowledge industry by specializing in information-related areas. In so doing, we also succeeded in establishing a corporate identity for our company. We have now completed the groundwork for our activities in the 1980s, based on a fundamentally C&C business outlook. I regard C&C as a long-term framework that should serve as a basis for our activities into the twenty-first century.

6. Human Factors in the Rise of C&C

At the beginning of 1980 I began to feel that it was time to go one step further with C&C. One thing that we must keep in mind, along with the technological factors, is the human factor of C&C. Human beings are the main actors who will be using and commanding data through the C&C medium. At the same time, they are, in every sense of the word, the principal developers of C&C. For this reason I used the phrase "Man and C&C" to represent the integration of computers and communications along a human axis.

Conventionally it has been necessary for operators of computers and communications to expend tremendous effort in adapting to a machine system in order to use it effectively. While we can say the amount of labor required has now been greatly reduced, it is still necessary to put considerable time into approaching and using sophisticated systems. Our ideal at NEC is to arrive at a more fulfilling social and cultural life through the use of information systems that anyone, not only specialists, can use quickly and easily.

The field that relies most on human labor is, as it turns out, software. Software production is presently burdened with serious problems—the so-called "software crisis." The world is unable to keep up with a burgeoning need to develop software. A rational development of the means of software production is crucial if C&C is to find its full potential.

The reduction of labor is made possible by both the enrichment of software, including more sophisticated machine languages, and by the advances in terminal design resulting from the addition of intelligence through the use of LSIs and VLSIs.

In other words, it can be seen as a measure of the advances in machine intelligence. I hardly need point out that this has been made possible by the progress in semiconductor circuit elements. By incorporating software based on human labor within these semiconductor circuit elements, we have succeeded in making the elements themselves intelligent.

7. Real-World Trends and Global Roles of C&C

While there may be some differences in the labels they use, those in electronics and many other well-informed people agree with the concepts of C&C and "Man and C&C," which I have just together by heavy reliance on information and knowledge gained of the twentieth century is likely to be the start-up of the C&C age. I perceive C&C following a steady development path as we move toward the year 2000.

That this is not merely speculation but a real trend in industrial society can be seen, for instance, in the adjustments in fields of business being made by the Bell system and IBM.

This is not only an inevitable consequence of technological progress, but also a response to the unavoidable need for any future industrial civilization—if it is to progress—to hold itself together by heavy reliance on information and knowledge gained from advances in C&C.

The world industrial map is now being redrawn around a new axis of information, knowledge, and the machinery they require. NEC has pursued telecommunications for more than eighty years since its founding. It has been involved in computers for more than thirty years and in semiconductor products for nearly as long. As a result I have been well placed to perceive relatively vividly and accurately this state of change. This is why I consider it the duty—and indeed the very rationale for existence—of my company to orient its future corporate concerns along the C&C growth path and to work to realize the concept's actual development.

Working along these three business axes, NEC is already actively developing new systems and products in anticipation of the C&C era. For instance, we have fiber-optic communications systems, satellite communications earth stations, digital switching systems, mainframe computer systems based on distributed information-processing network architecture (DINA), and personal computers. These products have already shown a solid performance in the global marketplace.

We have also recently succeeded in the practical development of VLSIs with memories in the 1-megabit range, and are working to create other high-level functional elements. This steady process can be seen a kind of warranty for the future development of C&C.

The advanced technology that came up for discussion in the Versailles Summit in France this past June as a tool for reactivating the world economy is, in the way it relies on new developments in electronics, basically the same as the C&C I advocate. When I met Herman Kahn during one of his recent visits to Japan, he praised the growing "information-intensive society" under way in Japan, and indicated that he understood C&C to be similar to his theoretical views on information and intelligence. C&C is not merely a corporate goal of NEC, it is now being universalized as one of the global trends of the era.

C&C has won recognition as a development that promises to reconstruct our civilization around knowledge and information. This is true not only for Japan, which lacks adequate natural resources and raw materials, but also for the entire modern world, where constraints on economic growth are increasing day by day. C&C can contribute mightily to conserving energy, reducing demands on raw materials, and enhancing the efficiency of every kind of system.

8. Concrete Examples: The User's Perspective

So far I have concentrated on introducing C&C and placing it in perspective from the developer and supplier's viewpoint. I have talked in terms of technological directions, and one might say I have described the scenery along the upper reaches of the great river called electronics. However, there is also a great and growing interest in the effects that C&C will have on the common citizen and society. There is a demand for predictions about what things will be like downstream. A general user's perspective is called for.

There are any number of institutions trying their hand at developing such future outlooks today in Japan, and the same is true in other countries as well. A number of quite difficult factors need to be taken into account in making such predictions. Nevertheless, I have decided to make such an attempt here, and I believe we cannot go too far wrong with my general overview.

First of all I believe that we can identify the areas for C&C applications according to their market characteristics: the public sector, the business sector, and the home sector. We can further divide the business sector into office and factory applications. Both the public and the business sectors can be conceptualized spatially at an international level as well as at a national or regional level.

The other important consideration is chronological. We can divide our three sectors further, based on what we can expect to see come about in the next few years, and on what may not take place until the year 2000. Taken all together, these market and chronological divisions form a matrix framework within which the many variations of C&C will develop.

One point I would like to emphasize is that, as the practical development of C&C continues, there will be a significant change in the way these systems are operated. Instead of a single enterprise being responsible for running these systems, we will see the rise of a multidimensional structure involving government, public organizations, and private industry—even hospitals, associations, and libraries—as the public and market dimensions of C&C make themselves felt. This will of course also include the multilayered development of broadcasting business on a par with so-called telecommunications enterprises. It will therefore become increasingly necessary for us to take into account this multilayered structure of C&C as it is seen from an operational perspective. This so-called C&C matrix structure is illustrated in Figure 3.

8.1 Grand Networks

Let us now turn to some specific predictions about C&C.

First, about grand networks. Grand networks are either wired or wireless. In wired systems we will see fiber optics taking over

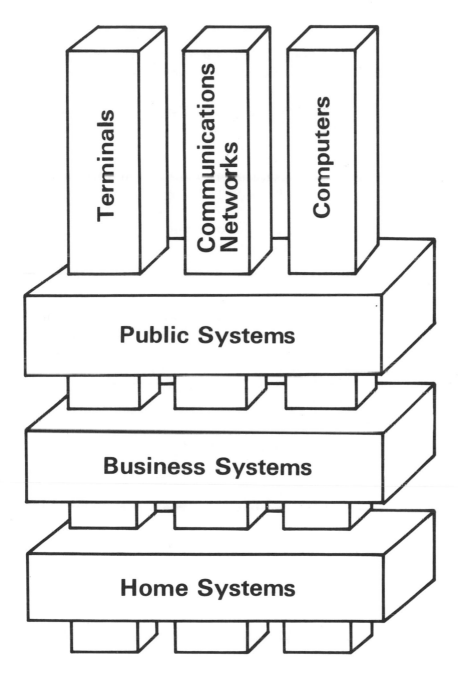

Fig. 3 The Matrix Structure of C&C

from the traditional cable circuits. Moreover, voice transmission will be supplemented by the transmission of data and characters, graphic and video information, all using digital coding. The establishment of this infrastructure will require from ten to twenty years, and is expected to take between $10 and $15 billion for a region with a population of between 50 and 100 billion.

In wireless systems, satellites will take center stage alongside the conventional microwave circuits, and will be used to put together communications and broadcasting networks. The question of whether satellite reception will be handled on a community or an individual basis is really more one of economics than technology.

The interstices of these networks will rely on an electronic switching system, which in addition to switching will provide answering services when the recipient is out or the line is busy, and a multiplicity of other user-tailored services. And of course, we can also predict the appearance of new terminals offering a full range of new functions to cope with the new networks.

Meanwhile, a host of dedicated satellites will no doubt be hard at work in the heavens, forecasting the weather, aiding maritime navigation, and fulfilling other specialized tasks. Also, mass media broadcasting will see increased interplay with its audiences as interactive systems make their appearance.

8.2 Knowledge-Processing Computers

My second example is in the computer field, where radical transformations in both form and function will entirely replace the current image of the mainframe computer. We cannot as yet accurately predict when we will see the commercialization of compound semiconductor elements and Josephson junctions. But even so, it is crystal clear that megabit VLSIs will become dominant in the future. We can further expect the old computer based on arithmetical calculation to evolve into an information-processing machine capable of making its own deductions. This development will permit us to speak at long last of machines that can stand in for many functions of the human brain, the kind of machines the general public looked forward to when computers first appeared. But I believe the biggest advance in computer functions will be that the computer will cease to be something that can be mastered only by a specialist armed with special training. Instead, anyone will be able to use computers simply by following a relatively simple set of procedures.

As equipment becomes more sophisticated, it will also become more compact, and there will be greater awareness of terminal configurations. The new terminals will no doubt reflect deeper consideration of human engineering needs.

8.3 From Personal Computers to Electronic Mailing Systems

My third example has to do with the compounding of personal computer functions.

Japan has only just begun to see the rapid spread of personal computers and Japanese-language word processors. Since Japan is not part of the alphabetic cultural sphere, we cannot dispense with ideographs. Given the number of characters required, a Japanese-language word processor is perhaps one hundred times more complex than its English counterpart. What seems likely therefore is that instead of waiting for improvements to be made in the performance of dedicated Japanese-language word processors, we will see Japanese-language word processing cropping up as one use for personal computers.

As this example shows, a steady cycle of improvements in the functions and performance of personal computers will lead them to share, or in some cases share out, the functions of the mainframe computers. Moreover, we can predict that through use with multiple interfaces personal computers will come to be numbered among the vital components of any C&C system.

I might also point out here that personal computers with word-processing functions will, along with facsimile terminals, also form the terminals of a future electronic mailing system.

Personal computers will almost certainly be linked into the grand networks I cited in my first example to create the third most important household electronics center after the telephone and the television receiver. When that happens it will be an easy matter technologically to outfit the home with all the equipment appropriate to the so-called "electronic cottage."

It is apparent that a similar situation is developing in many offices on a larger scale and much more quickly, thus promoting office automation.

8.4 Intelligent Robots

My fourth example is the progress and spread of intelligent robots. The robots that the Czechoslovakian playwright Karel Capek dreamed of in 1921 are now finally taking their first steps sixty years later, thanks to the progress and economics of microelectronics. Since these new machines have the direct effect of replacing human workers, controversy has arisen in recent years as to whether or not they will aggravate unemployment. However, I myself believe this is a battle of human versus robot wits, and I am convinced that humans must become wiser through the way they choose to use these new devices.

Robots should be employed in tasks that are dangerous or harmful to human health, or in jobs requiring extremely precise assembly. Meanwhile, we should work to shift human workers to higher-level jobs more suited to human qualities. I believe there is a tremendous need to devise ways for robots to develop resources discovered by earth-resource satellites. They have a clear role to play in ocean floor work, for example, and in many other tasks that can contribute to a more abundant human civilization.

8.5 Automatic Interpretation Telephone Systems

There is still a conspicuous lack of understanding among the peoples of the world. We in Japan feel particularly keenly that linguistic differences are a major barrier. Yet the languages of different nations are something that must be respected.

As my fifth example, therefore, I believe that in parallel with our understanding of C&C, the development of automatic interpretation telephone systems will be one of the indicators for the realization of the C&C concept. Fortunately we at NEC have at our disposal sophisticated voice-recognition and synthesis technologies that have been cultivated over twenty years. We hope· that by wedding these technologies to techniques of sentence

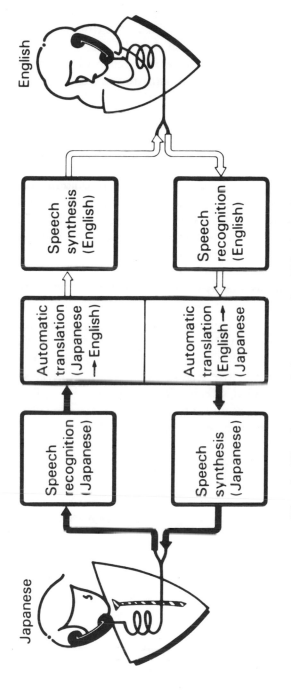

Fig. 4 The Automatic Interpretation Telephone System

analysis we will be able to achieve the dream of automatic interpretation. This would mean that if I were spoken to in English,
the meaning of the words would reach me in Japanese, and my
own thoughts would be transmitted to the other party translated
into English. Figure 4 depicts the procedures involved.

I have personally witnessed how ideas for a new technology—
be it pulse code modulation, geostationary satellites, or fiber-
optic communication—have been brought into practical use
through diligent human effort. I am quite confident, therefore,
that automatic interpretation telephone systems will be realized
before the year 2000. In fact I have made it my life goal to see
this come about, and I find myself encouraged in my efforts by
the thought that this marvelous technology will be the greatest
gift that C&C can bring mankind.

There is no end to examples of the coming C&C age. What
I have sought to do is point out that the distinctive characteristics
of C&C do not manifest themselves in the individual functions
of individual products. Rather we will find them in the compound
use of all these different functions together. I have also sought
to stress that healthy market needs should be our standard for
determining what effects C&C technologies will have, and for
setting the direction in which we should guide system and product development in response.

Thank you very much.

WORKS CITED

Bell, Daniel. *The Coming of Post-Industrial Society*. New York: Basic Books, Inc., 1973.

Burck, Gilbert. "Knowledge, the Biggest Growth Industry of Them All." *Fortune*, November 1964.

Clarke, Arthur C. "Extra-Terrestrial Relays: Can Rocket Stations Give World-Wide Radio Coverage?" *Wireless World*, October 1945.

Kobayashi, Koji. *C&C and Software*. The Simul Press, 1982.

———. *My Personal History: From the Mountains of Japan to the World Stage*. Tokyo, Japan: Nihon Keizai Shimbun, 1988.

———. "Digital Technology and the Advance of Automation." *OHM*, March 1959.

———. "The Impact of Space Technology and C&C." Speech at the American Association for the Advancement of Science, Washington, D.C., January 1982.

———. "The Japanese Computer Industry: Its Roots and Development." Keynote speech at the 3d USA-Japan Computer Conference, San Francisco, California, October 1978.

————. "Milestones and the Future Potential of the Electronics Industry in Japan." Speech at the 30th anniversary of the Japan Electronics Industry Development Association, Tokyo, Japan, May 1978.

————. "Shaping a Communications Industry to Meet the Ever-Changing Needs of Society." Keynote speech at Intelcom 77, Atlanta, Georgia, October 1977.

Machup, Fritz. *The Production and Distribution of Knowledge in the United States.* Princeton, N.J.: Princeton University Press, 1962.

Meadows, Donella H., Dennis L. Meadows, Jørgen Randers, and William W. Behrens III. *The Limits to Growth.* New York: Universe Books, 1972.

Naisbitt, John. *Megatrends.* New York: Warner Books, 1982.

Nakashima, Akira, and Masao Hanzawa "Algebraic Expressions Relative to Simple Partial Paths in Relay Circuits." *Journal of the Institute of Telegraph and Telephone Engineers.* Part 1, December 1936; part 2, February 1937 (in Japanese).

Petal, Marvin H. "Nippon Electric Does It the U.S. Way." *Business Week,* November 11, 1965.

Porat, Marc Uri. *The Information Economy: Definition and Measurement.* U.S. Department of Commerce, 1977.

Porter, Michael E. "The Nippon Electric Company, Limited." Case Study, Harvard Business School, Cambridge, Massachusetts, 1982.

Toffler, Alvin. *The Third Wave.* New York: W. Morrow & Co., 1980.

Toward the Establishment of Mutual Understanding Between Business and Society. Tokyo, Japan: The Japan Committee for Economic Development, 1973 (in Japanese).

U.S. Congress. House. Subcommittee on Trade of the Committee of Ways and Means. *High Technology and Japanese Industrial Policy: Strategy for U.S. Policymakers.* Report prepared by Julian Gresser. 97th Cong., 1980.

INDEX